GATHER NO MOSS

GATHER NO MOSS

SARAH SHEARS

Author of
Tapioca for Tea

PAUL ELEK BOOKS

ISBN.0.236.17694.3

Published in Great Britain by

PAUL ELEK BOOKS LIMITED

54-58 Caledonian Road, London N1 9RN

Printed by

Weatherby Woolnough Limited

Sanders Road, Wellingborough, Northants. NN8 4BX

CONTENTS

I

HOME

'A rolling stone gathers no moss', Mother said firmly.

'Who wants moss?' I retorted.

I had reached the age of thirteen when I discovered the reason for the awkwardness and restlessness of which I was often accused as a small child.

'It is a legacy from your father', I was told. 'You have inherited his temperament and wanderlust!' I received this information with much pride, I remember, since Father, who had died in Baghdad, had been a colourful figure whose rare visits had fired my young imagination.

There were four of us. William, Mary and Henry were all Mother's children. They had her steadfastness and contentment. I envied, but could not emulate them. My father's personality was strong in me, and grew stronger as the years went by.

In our remote Kentish village, in the early part of the century, the majority of boys leaving school at the age of fourteen had several alternatives—farm-work, gardening, or trade. The girls had no alternative, and their destiny was called, ironically, 'good service'. But Mother was not defeated by this village tradition, and planned for better things. In William she recognised the need of further education, so that he could qualify for a banking career. She realised that Mary's maternal instinct could only find satisfaction in children, but still needed a period of training and discipline first. In Henry, her youngest, she met with some opposition, for his earnest desire to *earn* a living was apparent from the age of nine! He was finally persuaded into a five-year apprenticeship to an expanding motor-bus company. To overcome my extreme reluctance to anything of a permanent nature, I was promised an interesting career as a post office clerk. Five years in the village post office, with a starting wage of five shillings weekly, a twelve-hour day, and no Bank Holidays, only served to prove my own definite conclusion that I was totally unfit for such a life. But there was no escape for anyone then, until they 'came of age'. At twenty-one, I did not ask for, or receive the key of the door, but demanded the right to expand and explore. Then, filled with remorse, apologised, and went back behind the counter! To compensate for my disappointment, however, I spent the entire legacy from Father, on a beautiful grand piano—much too beautiful and grand for Mother's cosy little front room. And I had no talent at all as a pianist, unfortunately. My one small talent—for writing—was despised and discouraged, and it was generally assumed that my stories and poems were a shocking waste of time and energy. Reading was another time-waster.

'You get absorbed in a book when stockings have to be darned, or somebody is waiting for hot cocoa!' Mother would scold.

'Your mind is so cluttered, Sarah, you should learn to discriminate,' said William loftily.

'Wait!', they told me, 'there is time enough to see the world.'

'Wait!', they told me 'you could still pass that Civil Service examination, and remember the pension at sixty!' But I was not listening. Father beckoned a ghostly finger, from the fabulous cities of Bombay and Baghdad. Time was short, and I was getting desperate.

'I must go!', I wept and pleaded. 'I must get away.'

'Then go!', said Mother, flaring up, 'but don't come running back, when you have spent all your money, or your plans don't materialise.'

'But I have no plans', I confessed.

'No plans! Then you must be mad!'

'If there is a pattern I shall find it, eventually. I just want to be free.'

'Free! Is anyone ever free?'

'Yes, Father was free.'

'He thought he was, but then he discovered his obligations had to be met. Freedom is really self-indulgence.' Her brown eyes were black with annoyance.

8

'Mother, I still have to go.'

She turned away. Her back was straight, but her mind and her will had been shocked into a situation identical to the one in 1920—when Father went away. Their personalities were too strong for unity, so conflicting forces drove them apart. Yet the forces were good, not evil: security as opposed to adventure; calmness to emotionalism; parochial contentment to an extravagant worldwide curiosity. It was just that I knew which forces were in me.

ABROAD

A copy of *The Times* spread over the post-office counter caught the postmaster's eye, and he frowned disapprovingly, for this was a rather select resort of Hove, in Sussex, not a remote country village in Kent. One male customer smiled at my impertinence, and invited me to join him for a coffee at a nearby restaurant, when I had finished with the paper!

But a lady customer reminded me tartly that I should be better employed attending to my post-office business.

'There is a time for everything, and this is no time for reading the morning paper,' agreed her companion, impatiently waiting to be served with a penny stamp.

'Take over, girls!' I instructed my two juniors, flippantly, 'I have an important letter to write,' and I retired to the private cubby-hole with a clean sheet of notepaper, and an envelope marked with the letters OHMS.

On His Majesty's Service? Well, hardly. The advertisement that had caught my eye requested that any young lady of English nationality, between the age of 20 and 25 years, devoted to small children, and willing to travel, should apply immediately to an address in The Hague, Holland. Interviews would be arranged in London.

It was so essentially *right* for me, I felt the impact of those printed words, and was quite incapable of ignoring them.

'Willing to travel'—not only willing, but eager and hungry for travel! 'Devoted to small children'—my natural affection for Mary, Henry and Jackie (our adopted brother) when they were little, could hardly be described as 'devotion', but I was not deterred by this thought, for I would obligingly devote myself to the most objectionable little monsters, providing I could accompany them on their travels!

My heart throbbed excitedly, and the pen trembled in my hand, but I compelled my wandering thoughts to concentrate on the letter of application. All my eagerness and enthusiasm for foreign travel and my devotion to the unknown children was poured on the page, and a copy of a reference enclosed.

Then a shiver of apprehension made me hesitate before sealing the envelope. Would a post-office clerk be considered a suitable candidate for such a very unusual engagement?

'Sarah looks as though she has lost a penny and found sixpence!' said one of the junior clerks cheekily, as I popped the letter in the post-box.

But I was not a born disciplinarian, and she knew it!

'Work should be enjoyed, not just tolerated,' I had told them one day. 'If you don't enjoy being a post-office clerk, then find something you do enjoy. The same can be said for a dustman, a road-sweeper, or a policeman!'

'Coo, lummy, whatever next?' retorted sixteen-year-old Sylvia. 'Whoever heard of enjoying work? I enjoy getting my pay-packet on Friday!'

'Me, too,' echoed Margot, who was saving every penny to get married.

They both knew I was longing to get away, forever, from the post-office counter, and would take the first opportunity.

'Good luck!' they chorused, when I told them about the advertisement, and Sylvia asked, inquisitively,—

'You wouldn't dare, would you?'

'Just wait and see!'

'What with all them foreigners, what can't speak a word of English?' shrieked Margot.

They too obviously thought I was more than a little mad!

Mother still insisted that security was the one essential ingredient to a happy and contented life, but the urge to escape from this bondage of security was as strong as ever in me.

'Good luck!' the girls had wished me, and good luck was Chance. It had nothing to do with security. All the years of home training, example and discipline seemed to have been wasted. I was still my Father's daughter, and his recklessness possessed me that day.

With a packet of sandwiches and an apple, I hurried down to the beach, to spend my lunch hour outdoors. Sitting on the hard pebbles, with the wind tearing at my hair—it was early

March—I felt my spirits soar beyond the horizon. The sandwiches were damp with spray and tasted of salt, and I sat there hugging my knees, seeing the dream about to be realised.

How soon should I hear? What should I wear for the interview? How would I get to The Hague? These thoughts occupied my mind almost exclusively, during the following week.

Automatically, from force of habit, I managed to serve the customers and to balance my accounts—but in spirit I was already in Holland.

*　　*　　*　　*　　*

'A letter for you, Sarah,—with a *foreign* stamp,' said Mother, suspiciously, one morning. (We had moved from our country cottage to a modern house in Worthing—when Mother received her share of Grandmother's legacy.)

I had been trying, for two whole weeks, to intercept the postman, but now the letter Mother had found on the doormat seemed to spark with vibrations, like a live object, as it passed from her hand to mine. She stood over me while I tore it open, watching my nervous fumbling. Scanning the letter hurriedly, I felt a hot, guilty flush on my face, and sensed her displeasure, even before I opened my mouth to speak. The moment for which I had alternately yearned and dreaded, had arrived. It could not be postponed. She knew already that I was simply following Father's footsteps, and that nothing could stop me now.

'It's from The Hague, in Holland. I answered an advertisement in *The Times* and I have an appointment for Thursday of this week.' My voice sounded flat and unemotional, for Mother stood there, searching my flushed face with her deep, dark eyes. Her mouth was grim and her face had paled. Then she began to collect the breakfast dishes from the table.

'Mother!—*please* try to understand,' I pleaded—but she had turned her back on me.

'I shall never understand you, if I live to be a hundred.'

It was her ultimatum. The filial bond which had bound us together was finally broken. It was the end of her supreme authority and the beginning of a new chapter for me. Yet, I felt only sadness and regret for causing her so much pain and disappointment. Torn apart, as always, by conflicting emotions, I was tempted to fling my arms about her neck, beg her forgiveness, promise her the one thing in the world she wanted of me—to fold my wings and settle down. Her displeasure and annoyance was hurtful; her complete lack of interest distressed me. I felt that she actually disliked me at that moment—yet I had never loved her so dearly.

Tears streamed down my face; chokingly I groped for the packet of sandwiches she had prepared for my lunch.

'I must go, I shall miss the train.'

She still had her back to me at the kitchen sink. I pressed my wet cheek to her dry one, and ran out of the room. It was the first time in my life she had refused to kiss me goodbye. This in itself was a punishment I found almost intolerable, in spite of my twenty-three years. Blinded by tears, I ran all the way to the station, still clutching the letter.

I was one of a selected list of six applicants, and my chances were good, but Mother's displeasure had destroyed all the satisfaction. Should I turn back, miss the train, and comfort her with my apologies and promises? She would be crying now at the kitchen sink. Her tears were always private. But still my feet hurried over the pavement, and the urge to go forward, not back, was strong and compelling.

The train was moving from the platform, and a hand came out to pull me into the last carriage. Sympathetic glances from my fellow travellers reminded me that I was still crying. The train gathered speed, and I sat there, in my cramped corner, wondering what devil possessed me, that I could behave so strangely, so contrary to Mother's wishes.

For the fascination of Chance, I had rejected the bondage of Security. An avid curiosity still possessed me and I had to look around the next corner. My hands closed over the letter. What should I wear for the interview? How do I get to The Hague?

*   *   *   *

'No, Miss Shears, it will *not* be convenient at all for you to take the day off on Thursday,' the postmaster declared emphatically.

'You have Saturday afternoon and Sunday for your private engagements.'

I was furious. It was so unexpected, and the two junior

clerks were quite capable of holding the fort for one day. But he picked up the telephone and dismissed me with a flip of the hand.

'He's an old misery!' Sylvia pulled a face. 'It's a shame you have to miss such a good opportunity.'

'I'm not missing it, I'm going after office hours!' I told them, and dictated a telegram to Margot.

'Regret not free to interview till early evening Thursday stop Please confirm if 7.30 convenient—Sarah Shears'

A few minutes before closing time the reply was phoned through to the office.

'Expect you Grosvenor House Hotel 7.30 Thursday— Wilhemina Van de Goort'

The girls hugged me excitedly, and even the boy-friends were kept waiting that evening. But I was reluctant to go home, and wandered along the sea-shore to stare once again at the Channel and the distant horizon. The sea was grey and I shivered in the keen wind.

'You cannot eat your cake and have it', I was told. But that is exactly what I wanted to do! To be free to wander, without any particular plan or purpose, yet, at the same time to please Mother, and to keep her love and respect. It was an impossible theory that I might be able to combine the two. In my heart I knew it was impossible, but like Mother I had never much cared for the word. But now, facing the future, with its inevitable loneliness and separation, I could share the same apprehension as Father, all those years ago. Mother would be as adamant now as she was then.

'But where will it get you? What will you gain by all this moving around?'

Reason had no answer to such questions and instinct was too vulnerable. But she would not fight any more, she would let me go. I could still hear the words she addressed to Father, that evening, long ago.

'*Then you go alone, and I stay here—and the children stay with me.*'

Whose was the victory, then—Mother's or Father's? I have never been able to decide. And I should walk alone from henceforth. Home would be nothing more than a lodging place for a traveller. This, then, was the legacy my Father had bequeathed to me, his eldest daughter—it was a solemn thought.

*   *   *   *   *

In spite of my recklessness, I was so nervous and apprehensive about the interview, I asked my current boy-friend, Tom, to meet me at Victoria. We had met at Grandmother's funeral and he was distantly related to me.

Tom was a surveyor, a sturdy, intelligent man of thirty, with his future planned as carefully and meticulously as he dressed. I knew he had been seriously considering an engagement, but now, when he was suddenly called to escort me to a Park Lane Hotel, to meet a prospective employer, from Holland, he had grave doubts.

'Holland?' he repeated, incredulously, when we had settled into the cab at Victoria. (Why a taxi, Sarah, when buses pass the door?)

'Yes, Holland—it just happened to be Holland, that's all—Hong Kong or Timbuktu would have done just as well!' I told him flippantly, to cover up the nervous tension rapidly mounting, as we sped towards my destination. 'Don't fuss, Tom, there's a dear. Hold my hand, please, I'm petrified!'

He took my hand, obligingly, but there was no warmth or comfort in the hand clasp.

'Are you actually considering taking a job in Holland?' he persisted.

I nodded vigorously, and my eyes swept over the crowded streets, and lovers on the seats in Hyde Park.

'And giving up the post-office?'

I nodded again. Tom was frowning with disapproval.

'Now don't *you* start to lecture me. I've had enough lectures in the past two weeks to last a lifetime!' I told him.

He relented a little when the taxi stopped at the imposing entrance to Grosvenor House and I waited impatiently on the kerb while he carefully counted out the fare, then, with the air of a man bestowing a great favour, added an extra threepence. Looking down at me, he seemed to consider I was still too young and innocent to enter such an establishment, unaccompanied by a strong escort.

'I'm coming with you.' He took my arm protectively.

'As far as the foyer, but no further, thank you, Tom.'

I gave him a fleeting, nervous smile, and he promised to wait for me.

'I shan't move from this spot, so don't hesitate to call on me if you need me,' he insisted, manfully.

I left him sitting there, looking very serious, and I knew he was wondering what to do about breaking off our brief attachment. Obviously he was puzzled and upset by such a surprising display of independence on my part, when I had allowed him to believe I was a nice, sensible girl, with few vices, other than a passion for coconut ice and doughnuts!

But I forgot his existence, for the next one and half hours, as completely as I forgot everyone I had ever known.

Stepping out of the lift, attended by a uniformed young boy, I stepped out of my old self, and left it behind, forever. Suddenly, all my nervousness had vanished, and a joyous expectation possessed me, so that I smiled at the boy, as he tapped on the door, and pressed a shilling into his hand.

'Thank you, Miss.' He seemed surprised and pleased, saluted smartly, and marched away.

A fair young woman, not much above my own age, slim and elegant in a tailored dress, greeted me charmingly, with outstretched hand.

'Good evening, Miss Shears. How nice of you to come. Do sit down. You must be tired if you have come straight from the office? Does that mean you missed your dinner altogether, this evening?'

I stared for a moment, and asked,

'Excuse me, but you *are* Mrs Van de Goort?'

'Yes, why, did you expect someone older?'

'I hardly knew what to expect, but you look so *English*— and you haven't a trace of an accent'

She laughed, delightedly.

'I am often mistaken for an English woman, but I assure you I am one hundred per cent Dutch!—and extremely proud of the fact. Now about your dinner. You must have something you poor dear.'

She picked up the telephone, and smiled reassuringly.

'Will coffee and sandwiches do?'

'Thank you very much,' I murmured politely. (She might have been a little surprised to see me with an evening 'dinner' of stew and dumplings or bread pudding solid with currants and candied peel, for Mother was a poor cook, and her dishes invariably stodgy!).

I was very impressed by my surroundings, though not over-awed. It was my first glimpse of a luxury hotel, and it seemed to me extremely elegant, but also extremely comfortable. The genuine warmth of the welcome, and the natural charm of her manner had dispelled everything but sheer enjoyment in the novel situation.

If Mrs Van de Goort had received all six applicants in the same way, then she must be a very nice person, I decided, and wondered whether she had yet engaged anyone.

When the tray was placed on a convenient table, beside my chair, the fragrant aroma of coffee, and dainty chicken sandwiches, reminded me I had had no lunch or tea that day—I was too excited. But now I was ravenously hungry. Real coffee was a luxury too, for it was too expensive to indulge in every day.

'Now take your time, for there is absolutely no hurry, and the rest of the evening is at our disposal,' my hostess insisted.

The grey eyes seemed amused, I thought, as she settled comfortably in the big armchair.

'Now let me do all the talking for the moment, you just concentrate on the sandwiches. Are they good?'

'Marvellous!'

'You look much younger than your twenty-three years, but I expect it's that lovely schoolgirl complexion,' she decided. 'What is the secret, I wonder? Look at me now—pasty as an underdone pancake!'

I laughed indulgently, and took another bite of chicken sandwich. I knew she was observing me closely, but I felt her scrutiny to be kind and tolerant, rather than critical.

'I have seen the other five applicants today, but I couldn't make up my mind on any one of them,' she confessed. 'They all had excellent qualifications and references, common sense, good breeding, in fact everything but the one thing I was looking for.' She gave me a shrewd glance and went on. 'Now I know *you* have a sense of humour, Miss Shears, it was apparent from the moment you walked into this room. I felt you were not putting on an act for my benefit, but really enjoying yourself,—am I right?'

'Absolutely!' I chuckled, and sipped the hot fragrant coffee.

'A sense of humour is a priceless gift,' she insisted. 'Now I must explain more fully, for the advertisement was rather vague —at least my husband thought so. I am not looking for a trained nanny, or a qualified nursery governess. My two children, Mathilde, aged six, and Mark, aged three, speak English perfectly, for they had a Norland nanny from birth. They also speak and understand a little German, for we have a German cook. But that is not at all clever, Miss Shears. It's perfectly natural in young children.'

'Not in this country, Mrs Van de Goort.'

She shrugged.

'No, perhaps not, but then the English are so certain of finding someone to speak their own language in almost any country of the world, they don't bother. It makes them a little conceited and lazy! Now, how many people would you en- counter speaking Dutch; unless you happened to visit South Africa, or the Dutch East Indies?'

'Very few, I imagine.'

'Exactly. We need another language every time we cross the frontier into Germany or Belgium. That is why we consider languages so important in our education system. English is taught even in the kindergarten, and French and German from the age of nine or ten. We are advanced in some ways, but quite Victorian in others,' she smiled, whimsically. 'Family life, for instance, in our class of society, still follows more or less the same pattern as in grandmother's day. We have our drawing rooms, and our children spend an hour with their parents after tea. This is traditional, but they are not banished to nurseries, as in England. Once they have reached the age of three, they have meals in the dining room with their parents, go visiting, and have holidays elsewhere in Europe. The girls in the family are taught all the social graces at a 'finishing school' in Switzerland. We get married, and thereafter live rather dull and conventional lives that suit us admirably!'

I listened attentively to her description of a life so different from our own. It had a flavour of gracious bygone days and leisurely old-world charm. Mathilde and Mark would be delightful children with nice manners, and I should not have to try very hard to like them. But would they like me?

'My husband and I thought a 'children's companion' would be the answer, at this stage, now they have both outgrown a nanny,' Mrs Van de Goort continued. 'An English girl for a year or so, then a French mademoiselle, followed by a German fraulein. This would ensure English, French and German conversation in turn—for the children would be allowed to speak Dutch *only* when they were not accompanied by the young companion. Does that seem a sensible arrangement?'

'It seems to me an excellent idea,' I agreed.

She leaned forward, and asked, eagerly,—

'Then, you will come?'

'I should love to!' I told her, without a second's hesitation.

She laughed at my enthusiasm, and assured me gaily, 'I think the children will like you!'

* * * * *

It was nine o'clock when she looked at her watch, 'But I must not keep you any longer, or your Mother will be getting alarmed.'

We had talked for an hour and a half!

I had heard all about the large family of relatives visited at week-ends, and that she planned to spend the whole of the two months' summer vacation in Switzerland.

'My husband will join us for two weeks in August, and then we shall have to behave ourselves, and stay in the best hotels!' she chuckled.

They lived in the residential part of The Hague, had a car, a dachshund, two maids, a cook and a gardener. I should have a pretty bed-sitting room at the top of the house, and freedom to invite my English friends, from the English Church. Perhaps I should like a cheque to cover my expenses? And could I be ready to start in about ten days or so . .?

* * * * *

It was all too good to be true, and I walked in a daze across the foyer, clutching a cheque for ten pounds.

'Hi! . . remember me?'

Tom started up abruptly, and folded the evening paper. He was yawning with boredom and very short with me.

'Well, I don't need to ask, your face gives me the answer,' he said, gloomily, as we went out. 'Not another taxi?' he groaned, as I waved my hand at a stationary cab.

'I'm paying this time, Tom, old dear!' I showed him the cheque. '*And* I'm to be paid £25 *English* pounds per month, *and* I am going to spend all the summer in Switzerland!' I giggled excitedly as I climbed into the cab.

Tom was too stunned to reply, and sulked all the way to Victoria.

'Well, take care of yourself. I don't suppose I shall see you again.'

It was more of a statement than a question, for I was sure he had decided I would make a most unsatisfactory wife.

As the train moved away I leaned out and kissed him.

'I'm sorry, Tom, but I have to be free. Thank you for meeting me, and for being so patient.'

His face slid away. He was smiling and waving now, as relieved as myself to be spared a scene on the station platform. He was so nice, so reliable, so sure of himself and his future prospects.

I never saw him again, but I heard years later that he had a most successful career, a big house at Highgate, an attractive wife, and four lovely children.

But then Tom had a plan and a purpose in life, and I had none!

*   *   *   *   *

'Take the train from Liverpool Street to Harwich, then the boat from Harwich to Flushing. At Flushing your baggage will be examined, and your passport. You then take the train to The Hague, where we shall meet you in the car. That's simple enough, isn't it? I am sure you will manage it without any difficulties at all.'

I repeated Mrs Van de Goort's directions parrot-wise, like a passage of scripture in the village school. But now it seemed no longer an easy journey to The Hague, but a frightening and nerve-racking prospect, alone. If I had been travelling to Hong Kong or Timbuktu I could not have been more uncertain of the route.

The parting with Mother and the family had completely shattered my confidence again, for they had all shown their disapproval, and in one way or another had indicated that I was more than a little mad.

Sitting alone and forlorn in an empty carriage, en route to Victoria, with two new suitcases on the rack, and a new passport in my handbag, the first taste of freedom and independence was bitter as gall.

The joy and excitement I had anticipated was a mere figment of the imagination. There was no joy and excitement in this lone adventure—nothing in the world to compensate for the anguish on Mother's face and the appeal in her dark eyes. I was a monster of selfishness—an outcast, I told myself—and opened the new passport. The young woman in the photograph was a stranger, with her plump cheeks and staring eyes.

But for the first time in my life I could travel comfortably. Porters to carry my luggage, and taxis to convey me from station to station. I had experienced the ease and novelty of taxi travel for the first time that memorable evening with Tom. Misgivings about my casual treatment of him almost persuaded me that I had made a sad mistake.

'He was so sensible, so reliable, and his future prospects so good,' Mother had reminded me.

Dear Tom! Perhaps I should make amends, write to him, and explain that I had this terrific urge to spread my wings, but only for a year. Then I should settle down. But a stab of dismay disproved the theory. How could I bear his distressing habit of counting and checking every penny he spent? How could I live with anyone so *mean*? Carefulness was a virtue, but meanness a vice.

No, it was better to make a clean break, for Tom would be content with nothing less than a formal engagement, then marriage a year or two later. That would be bondage again— a lifetime of bondage. Tom was so sure, so *smug*. He would never know this madness and misery of hovering between the two worlds of conviction and uncertainty, of pain and pleasure, of Mother's opposition and my own inherent curiosity for life. Goodbye Tom: the brief attachment was over and I must walk alone.

*   *   *   *   *

Liverpool Street Station was dark, dirty and dreary, but it had no time to depress me, for I was whisked away on the fourth stage of my journey. Now I sat in the dining-car, awaiting my first meal on a train, another luxury for me. I ordered steak and chips, chocolate ice-cream and coffee. The novelty of lunch on the train, the appetising food, and the pleasant waiter soon revived me. Hunger is a disquieting state, and I had had no breakfast and had scarcely touched food for several days.

The small individual table gave me a feeling of superiority, for I could observe my fellow travellers without the effort of conversation. I was not yet ready to converse with strangers.

So far, the journey had been easy and quite uneventful, apart from the novelty. But Harwich was also dark, dirty and dreary, and the little harbour so desolate that I wondered how all the visitors to our shores would feel as they disembarked there.

But now it was a steward who welcomed me with a smile, and directed me to what he called a 'state-room'. My dormant sense of humour emerged to enjoy this flattering description of so dreary a compartment! It reminded me of the saloon bar in the cowboy films we had seen in the village hall, with its flickering gaslight, and rows of bottles, and customers lolling on the counter. Red plush seats and mahogany tables completed the illusion of grandeur.

'A cup of tea, please.'

The other customers were having something stronger. The tea was well stewed and sweet as syrup. It was served in thick cups boldly marked GER.

'Great Eastern Railway,' the steward explained, in answer to my puzzled look. My smile was probably a little wan and wistful, for the 'state-room' was beginning to rock, and the bottles to rattle.

'Have a drink. Do you good, too much tea rots the stomach!' one of the customers suggested, boisterously.

'No thank you.' I staggered away upstairs.

Reeling across the deck, I watched the tea spill over into the saucer, and it revolted me. My stomach heaved. Clutching the rail with one hand, the black letters, GER, began to dance on the thick cup like marionettes before my swimming eyes.

'Mother!—Oh, Mother! I'm so *miserable!* I wailed inwardly. The grey sea mocked me with its callous indifference.

'I shouldn't stay here if I were you. It's going to be a rough crossing. Come below and lie down.'

The face under the peaked cap was kind and fatherly. He took my arm, and I looked once more at the dim receding outline of the harbour; then went below.

As we passed the open door of the state-room, a whiff of sausages and fried onions caught me unprepared. My escort murmured,

'You poor kid, you are not a very good sailor, are you? First door on the left. Take it easy.'

*   *   *   *   *

Flushing Station was bright and beautiful, with gleaming express locomotives, bound for the French and Italian Riviera. The Purser had not deserted me at the moment of disembarkation, but escorted me personally through the Customs sheds; found the ticket office, and finally put me on the train for The Hague.

'Feeling better?' he asked kindly, from the platform.

'I feel fine now, thanks to you!'

His slow infectious grin was warm and encouraging. He had found a corner seat for me in a crowded carriage. Now I was a 'foreigner', and the babble of strange tongues was confusing.

'Here comes a trolley. I'll get you some coffee—*real* coffee! And you must taste these hot, savoury rolls. They really are good. I can recommend them.'

'Thank you—but please let me pay.'

He had already provided me with magazines, and it was getting a little embarrassing, to see a stranger emptying his pockets.

Yet *was* he a stranger? To me, he was a friend, and the last link with England.

The window was pushed down, and coffee and rolls handed in, while the other passengers crowded to the window. Ten minutes later, the last familiar face, with its wide grin, slid away, and I sat down in my corner, to look about me dubiously. My anxious glances were met with beaming smiles and nods.

'You are English—and you are a *leettle* frightened, maybe, yes? It means nozing, mein fraulein. All is goot!' a large, benevolent lady assured me, and bit hungrily into her roll.

The other seven passengers all smiled and nodded agreement. They could all speak a little English, but I had, as yet, only two or three words of Dutch in my limited vocabulary. I carried an English/Dutch grammar in my handbag.

'Dank U wel,' I murmured, to prove I was no idiot!

A storm of praise and congratulations broke over me. Such cleverness! And my first visit too!

Then we settled down to enjoy our rolls and the journey passed quickly and pleasantly in such cheerful company.

*   *   *   *   *

'So here you are at last!'

Mrs Van de Goort's voice accosted me, as my eyes swept the crowd on the platform at The Hague. Her husband was introduced, and he bowed, formally, over my hand. He was tall, dark and distinctive, but unsmiling and somewhat formidable.

It was late evening now, and I had been travelling since early morning. The sleek car purred through the strange, beautiful city.

I had arrived!

Mathilde and Mark (dressed by Daniel Neal) stood waiting, side-by-side in the dining room, at precisely eight o'clock, the following morning.

Mathilde was plump and pretty, with fair ringlets and a bow in her hair. Mark, at three, an exact replica of his father, with glossy black hair and bold black eyes. They were both solemn, and shook hands politely, when formally introduced by their mother. Father seemed satisfied with their performance, and we all sat down to breakfast, with Mark next to me.

The maid came in quietly with coffee and toast, followed by the cook, with three plates on a tray—bacon, egg and fried bread, for the children and myself.

The cook, Marthe, was short and plump, the maid, Joanna, tall and heavily built, with a strong face. She was obviously proud of her English conversation, but not permitted to linger, for the master of the house was impatient to say Grace and get on with the meal.

Mark's dark eyes searched my face with a penetrating

stare, then he manfully tackled the fried egg on its tiny square of bread. It broke and spread over his plate. His face clouded with annoyance, and he slammed down the knife and fork, and made some remark in his mother tongue. Mrs Van de Goort flushed uncomfortably, but said nothing. Apparently only Father could deal with such emergencies?

'*Mark Anthony!*You will speak *English*, if you please—and you will hand your plate to Miss Shears, who will tidy up that revolting mess, and cut up your bacon.'

'Ja, Papa.'

'Mark!'

'*Yes*, Papa.'

The plate was pushed towards me. Father then ignored my frantic efforts to gather the egg on to the bread, and turned to his wife, to discuss a more interesting topic—in English.

'Did you thank Miss Shears?'

His manner now was suave; his voice soft and smooth, and I disliked him intensely.

Mark was such a little fellow, and only recently parted from the Norland nurse he had known and loved for the whole of his short life. He naturally resented me as a substitute for this kind, familiar person, and I could understand the child's resentment. Mathilde had apparently accepted the change with placid indifference. Her golden curls framed her dimpled face. Father had smiled, approvingly, in her direction, but scowled at the small boy, and waited.

'Thank you, Miss Shears.'

The perfect diction, to me, a stranger of very limited education, was remarkable. Like his parents and sister he spoke English with easy assurance. I might have been sitting with an English family in the class we had known as the 'Gentry', but for the child's brief lapse into his mother tongue.

This first meal with the family, and the stern 'Victorian' parent, was certainly a strain. I hoped the impeccable behaviour of the breakfast table would not be enforced all the time. Mrs Van de Goort, sensing my discomfort, and sympathy for the small boy at my side, smiled encouragingly across the table.

'Tomorrow morning you can help the children to dress, and bring them down at 7.45 a.m. That will give you a good start.'

We exchanged a glance of mutual understanding, and I was much relieved.

Both parents, I noticed, ate several slices of thin toast, and each slice was spread with a different variety of cheese, ham and liver sausage, smoked meat, all in paper-thin slices, as well as honey cake.

We had all finished our breakfast, and sat patiently waiting for Mark to drink his milk. His mouth was rimmed with cream, so I hastily wiped it with the starched white napkin tied around his neck.

'I wipe my own mouth,' he protested, snatching at the napkin.

The Father's smouldering eyes seemed to penetrate the child's averted face, for it flushed a rosy pink, and the stubborn little mouth trembled. But still he would not look at that stern parent at the head of the table, but caught his Mother's adoring glance. A mischievous glint danced in his dark eyes. He turned to me, and said, provocatively,

'I'm a big boy now!'

It was so essentially English—so exactly what Henry and Jackie would have said at the same age, I would have hugged him, but for the Father's disapproval.

At last the children were permitted to leave, and dutifully kissed their Father's cheek. Mathilde took my hand as we climbed the stairs. Her dimpled smile was sweet, her china blue eyes stared fixedly at my face.

'Do you like me?' she asked coaxingly. 'And do you think I am pretty?'

'I like you very much, Mathilde, and I think you are pretty.'

She seemed satisfied.

Mark marched ahead, leading the way to the bathroom. He was already fiddling with the buttons of his short, grey knickers.

'I do it myself,' he informed me, in a loud clear voice.

In the hall below, I saw his father's hands spread in a gesture of despair, and heard the mother's soothing voice. A black homberg was jammed angrily on the dark, smooth head; he snatched a cane from the hall stand, and pulled on a pair of yellow gloves. Impeccably dressed, unsmiling, the master of the house departed.

As the door closed behind him, I felt the old house sigh

with relief, and the kitchen door burst open. The flaxen-haired German cook, Marthe, poured out a torrent of words in her native tongue. Mrs Van de Goort laughed, delightedly, and they went back to the kitchen together.

The maids were stripping the beds, sheets, blankets, pillows, and mattresses, were piled on tables and chairs at the wide-flung windows.

'Spring-clean?' I asked, tentatively.

They both looked puzzled, then appealed to Mathilde, who translated my enquiry a little haughtily, I thought. Turning to me, she explained briefly.

'They do it every day.'

The second maid, Wanje, who spoke no English, was grey-haired and worried, but Joanna very anxious to talk to me, and oozing good nature.

'I make vere goot Eenglish van der Eenglish nurse,' she informed me proudly.

'Your English is *not* good, Joanna,' said Mathilde scornfully, tossing her curls.

The woman's face clouded with disappointment, like a child's.

'You .. are .. very .. clever .. Joanna. I .. speak .. only .. two .. words .. of Dutch!' I explained carefully.

Joanna was appeased and grateful, but I could make no contact at all with Marthe or Wanje. What a barrier it could be, this strangeness of tongue?

Mark had locked himself in the bathroom.

'I go get him,' said Joanna.

I heard her coaxing voice at the bathroom door, and Mark's voice rather shrill and excited from within. Mathilde wriggled beside me,

'I can't wait, Mark is *such* a nuisance, I shall tell Papa.'

A little diplomacy seemed to be called for at this stage, and I joined Joanna at the bathroom door.

'Mark! will you *please* come and help me, I can't manage without you.'

We heard him climbing on the stool, and the bolt slid back. He stood in the doorway—a rather arrogant small boy, with a determined air. Mathilde pushed passed him, and lifted her short, pleated skirt.

'Mathilde has not got a little dickie. She has only got a

bottomus,' Mark explained gravely, and added, for my benefit, should I still be in doubt—'*She's* a girl!'

* * * * * *

'I walk on the outside of the pavement,' Mark insisted,
'because it's dangerous.'

We had left Mathilde at her school, and now I had the
little boy as an escort for the morning walk. His moods were
variable as the weather, and he was determined we should
both ride on a *tram!* This adventurous spirit suited me admirably, but I was very much a novice, and had not enquired
of his mother whether it was permitted. Perhaps his Norland
nurse had taken him for a tram ride sometimes, as a treat?
I knew that he was still resentful, and spoke of her as though
he expected her back, after a short holiday. I had decided
it would be better to humour him for a few days, when we
were out together, away from the house, for I dreaded
a scene in the street, with this strong-willed little boy.
So he took my hand and hurried me along at a furious
pace.

The street was wide and straight, and divided into sections,
for motor traffic, pedestrians and cyclists. But everyone seemed
to be riding a bicycle—not only men in cloth caps and baggy
trousers but distinguished-looking gentlemen in black suits
and hombergs. Old and young, well-dressed and shabby,
they pedalled along the highway.

'What a lot of bicycles!' I exclaimed, as we turned into
another tree-lined avenue, with tram lines on the edge.

'If we meet the Queen, we stand still and bow, like this,'
said Mark, demonstrating for my benefit, on the edge of the
kerb.

'Does the Queen ride a bicycle, then?'

'Of course—everybody rides a bicycle. Papa rides a bicycle.
Mummy rides a bicycle, everybody rides a bicycle,' he insisted.

What fun, I thought, if we meet the Queen! But we heard
later in the day that she had taken Princess Juliana to the
Summer Palace for the Easter vacation, so Mark had to wait
several weeks for the privilege of bowing to his Queen.

A tram rattled towards us, and the child's eyes shone with
excitement. He had not the slightest doubt in his small head
that I should be able to cope with such a situation, on my

first morning in Holland! If Papa Van de Goort objected to his son riding on a public tram I had the excuse of being ignorant of such matters.

We climbed aboard.

A group of fishwives in national costume filled one end of the tram with their wide black skirts and enormous winged bonnets. We squeezed in beside them. Mark was clutching my hand a little nervously now.

'Where are we going?' I asked him, searching my purse for a guilder.

'I don't know.' His eyes were wide and puzzled.

'Does the conductor speak English?'

'I don't know.'

His three-year-old courage had deserted him. What happens now, I wondered.

The conductor stood waiting for the fares, so I took a deep breath and recited.

'Please . . we . . want . . only . . a . . little ride . . on the tram and we . . walk back.'

The fishwives tittered, the other passengers glanced up in surprise, and the conductor pushed his cap to the back of his head and muttered, 'Eenglish!'

'Mark, tell the conductor, *please* darling,' I coaxed. Everyone stared, waiting for the child to speak. Blushing with embarrassment he apparently translated my recital into Dutch.

Conductor and passengers all seemed to be exclaiming together at his cleverness, for his blushing spread, and he buried his face in my breast. Everyone was interested and amused by our short excursion and I received a few coins in exchange for the guilder with smiles.

We alighted at the next stop to a chorus of 'Goodbye! Goodbye!'

Somewhat relieved to find ourselves back on the same highway, we started on the homeward walk. Mark was quiet and solemn now, dragging his feet on the last lap.

'I don't like it when you speak English on the tram. Will you never learn to speak Dutch?' he asked, plaintively.

Both Mother and Father were horrified to hear of our short escapade and I was obliged to apologise, and to remember in future to take a 'nice little walk' with the children, or, in an emergency, to take a taxi—never a tram!

As the weeks went by I was still desperately homesick at certain times of the day. Mother wrote frequently and I posted a long letter to her every Sunday evening.

With so many new experiences I should have been satisfied, but my heart ached for the sound of Mother's voice, and a glimpse of the dear familiar faces of William, Mary, Henry and Jackie. I seemed to belong neither to the family, nor the servants, but somewhere in between. The loneliest time of the day, for me, was the 'drawing-room hour' after tea, when the children joined their parents, and the servants retired to the kitchen to gossip. I used this social hour to study my Dutch/English grammar, but progress was slow for the family spoke English all the time in my presence.

My one free day in the week, when I travelled by tram to the city, was the only opportunity to practise my elementary Dutch. I purchased stamps, stationery, stockings, soap—and coconut ice! Invariably my halting Dutch was quickly translated into perfect English by a post-office counter clerk, a shop assistant, or even a tram conductor. Everyone was so kind and willing to help, that I felt I should never learn! Mrs Van de Goort expressed some concern over my strange pronunciation: it was, in a sense, like a London Cockney, she explained, and not at all *nice*!

It was fun to sit at a pavement café, drinking coffee or hot chocolate, watching the people of a strange city, and listening to the gutteral tongue I found so difficult to imitate. To my surprise the congregation at the English Church in The Hague was mostly a Dutch one and I made no English friends during the eighteen months I lived there. After all, it seemed to be lacking in imagination to spend my precious free days shopping, gossiping and drinking tea with other English girls.

My regular 'dates' with an interesting and intelligent young man from Hilversum were not disclosed to my employers. He sat beside me in church one Sunday evening, and shared my hymn book. Thereafter, he never bothered to take one. We visited museums and art galleries at Amsterdam, the docks at Rotterdam, the islands in the Zuider Zee, and the bulb fields. We spent long summer evenings drifting down the canals in little pleasure steamers crowded with families, and I recognised the flat landscape I had seen in the old pictures on the classroom walls at the village school. Windmills and fields of tulips, little boys in baggy breeches, and toy houses with red roofs, red shutters and red gates. But Willy also insisted on improving his English, so my chances of improving my Dutch were negligible!

Family life at the Van de Goorts, in some respects, had a Victorian flavour. An old-world regimen had survived and Mathilde and Mark grew up in this sheltered environment. The only visitors to the house were relatives—aunts, uncles and cousins called on the Hague family from all parts of Holland, and the visits were returned, promptly and punctually.

When the parents came down to breakfast they stood in the doorway waiting for the children to greet them. Mathilde would obediently slide off her chair, say her dutiful 'Good Morning' and lift her dimpled cheek for a kiss. Mark, as always, was erratic and moody. Sometimes he would pretend to ignore his parents completely, but the blush gave him away, as he furiously shovelled food into his mouth. The atmosphere then was electric! But the child was still too young to win these constant battles, and his defiance would crumble with the curt reminder—'Mark Anthony! We are waiting.'

The 'drawing-room hour' was often disturbed in the same way, and Mark would be pushed out, yelling furiously, followed by the stern command—'Go to your room!'. I would watch from the top landing, as the small boy slowly climbed the stairs, sitting down on every third step to yell louder, and kick the banisters. '*Mark Anthony*!' The thunderous voice in the hall below would send him scampering into the old nursery, where I would find him huddled over his red engine, sobbing hysterically. Hardly a day passed without this enforced obedience. From my position as observer I continued to dislike the boy's father, while I became fond of the calm, sweet-tempered woman who was married to such an exacting martinet. Yet she adored him, and in his own peculiar way he adored her.

*　　*　　*　　*　　*

'We shall travel overnight on the train, stopping at Cologne, and eat our breakfast in Switzerland,' said Mrs Van de Goort, with the casualness of a seasoned traveller. She had been to London again, to buy more clothes for the children, and replenish her own wardrobe at Harrods. I had asked her to buy me two cotton frocks—but not at Harrods! On her return she insisted I should accept them both as a gift. This was embarrassing, for Mother's strict training reminded me I should not ask favours of people.

Papa Van de Goort was left on the platform at The Hague. As soon as the tall immaculate figure had vanished from our sight, we were just four children on a picnic—a picnic to last six weeks!

'Mummy, can I sleep on top and Shearie on my bottom?' Mark enquired blandly.

His mother's eyes crinkled with laughter, and she snatched off her hat and gloves, squeezed my shoulders affectionately. In her green linen dress, she looked very young and unsophisticated—almost like a sister. Not a word had been said, but the sense of relief and release was tremendous. The strain of being constantly on our best behaviour, had been, for me, more than a little tedious! Immediately we began to play 'I Spy' from the windows.

Some time later a steward staggered in with a pile of sheets and blankets to make up the bunks. In the confined space we managed to wash ourselves at a tiny corner basin, no bigger than a mixing bowl.

The train rushed and swayed on through the night. Mathilde was soon fast asleep in the next compartment. Mark sitting up near the ceiling, over my head, wide-eyed, flushed with excitement.

'It's the fastest train in the whole world,' he concluded, with great satisfaction.

As thrilled and excited as the child, I lay awake, for I couldn't bear to waste the night sleeping. First experiences can never be repeated, or the novelty recaptured. Every restless pulse was gratified now with this tearing pace.

'Shearie—are you 'sleep?' enquired a drowsy voice overhead.

'No—are you?' What a ridiculous question!

'You can come upstairs if you like—I'll let you.'

The invitation was too appealing to refuse. It was all part of the unconventional journey and the release from a dominant parent.

In the compartment next door the mother's long flaxen pigtails mingled with the child's curls, on the top bunk.

I climbed up, gathered the small warm body into my arms,

and he slept like a baby till dawn. It was all that I needed—
somewhere to go—and someone to love.

We were to stay at the Pension Gretelwald, on the outskirts
of a small village overlooking the lake of Thun in the Bernese
Oberland.

'It will be an unspoilt, unsophisticated sort of place, and the
children can run wild. We can have day excursions on the
lake, visit Interlaken, and take picnic lunches every day.
You will enjoy every moment, and so shall I, for there is
no place in Europe quite like Switzerland,' my companion
informed me.

The sun was hot on our bare heads, but mountain peaks
in the distance were snow-capped, as we climbed into the
station 'buggy'. Everything was clean and fresh and sweet-
smelling. We breathed the sparkling air ecstatically, and sang
a little song, to the tune of the rattling wheels.

'The grand old Duke of York,
He had ten thousand men,
He marched them up to the top of the hill,
And he marched them down again!'

Then we came to a steep hill and the horse refused to move,
We must all get out and walk, the old cabby explained with
a shrug. So our luggage rode up the hill and we walked alongside. It was a breathtaking view, as we climbed higher and
higher.

One side of the narrow road sloped gently through a dark
pine forest to the edge of the lake. The water had the shining
transparency of blue glass, while above the snow-capped
mountain peaks had the remote grandeur of unattainable
heights. Chalets perched on the hillside, their balconies
draped in scarlet geraniums, and cowbells tinkled in the
distance from meadows bright with flowers. My throat tightened, it was so incredibly beautiful.

The welcome was warm and exuberant at the Pension
Gretelwald, for it was a family concern, with father, mother
and two sturdy sons, (who joined the militia at week-ends,
for compulsory training) and two plump and pretty daughters.
They ran from all directions to greet their guests and show
us our rooms.

Our rooms were clean and bare as monk's cells, with floor boards scrubbed white, and beds draped in old-fashioned white quilts. The sun spilled over everything. It was a simple, enchanted place.

The other guests, of mixed nationality—I turned out to be the only English person—lay sprawled in the meadow among the flowers, or sat at little tables in the beer garden.

Mark was only interested in the cowbells.

'Our cows don't ring bells,' he said, obviously puzzled and curious to inspect them at close quarters. He was nearly four years old now, and constantly on a voyage of discovery. I took his hand, and we wandered away together.

*   *   *   *   *

The homesickness I had known in Holland became nothing more than momentary pangs of nostalgia in Switzerland. Perhaps I lived more fully, mentally and physically on the heights, whereas Holland was so flat. This flatness, to me, was unhealthy, for it deprived me of the natural energy and vitality derived from the years in the Weald of Kent. This strange lassitude I had known in The Hague was now revealed as nothing more than a natural result of a drastic change of environment.

'But of course environment affects your health,' the children's mother reminded me, knowledgeably.

But I hadn't known. Like Mark, I was constantly on a voyage of discovery.

'I could see you were wilting in The Hague, but could do nothing about it,' she confessed.

'Was it so obvious?'

I was ashamed, for I hadn't intended to wilt, whatever the circumstance, or environment. One week in the fresh, invigorating air of Switzerland, and I recovered all my energy and appetite.

The hills were steep for climbing, almost precipitous in places, but every day found the children more able to cope with the long day excursions we planned around the lake of Thun. They were glowing with health and vitality. Mathilde was a different child—a happy, boisterous little girl without the pouting and preening.

The relationship was not that of mother, children and

paid companion, but rather of four children, with the same light-hearted and tireless enjoyment of each passing hour. It was, for me, a revelation, but for my much-travelled friend, only what she had anticipated.

We woke to the tinkle of cowbells, the strong yodelling voice of Joseph, and the glowing face of his sister Berthe, in a white starched apron, pouring tea from a white teapot into white tea cups. It was this incredible whiteness that so impressed me—the snow on the mountains, the quilts and the floor-boards of our bedrooms, the aprons of mother and daughters, and the daisies in the meadows. Padding across the bare floor-boards, already warmed by the sun, I would fling open the balcony doors, to stand, for a moment of renewed wonder, in the breathtaking panorama of mountains, lake and pine forest, until the children joined me, in their cotton pyjamas, running, barefoot, to welcome the new day.

The simple breakfast of rolls, butter and black cherry jam, served with coffee, on the sunny balcony, seemed like a banquet, and we all ate ravenously and demanded more. Yet only an hour or so later, we would be raiding the haversack I always carried on my back, for packets of Toblerone chocolate. Time was something regulated not by clocks and watches, but by the warmth of the sun and the state of our appetites. We slept when we were tired and ate when we were hungry. It was as simple as that.

They were no longer creatures of habit and custom, these children and their mother, from a genteel society, but creatures of impulse and imagination—or so they seemed to me, in those few short weeks we spent together. They talked with strangers, forgot the stiff formalities with which they had been surrounded and ignored most of the conventions.

Although I dutifully sent postcards to all my friends and relations, I could not seem to share with them the rapture I was feeling, or the warmth and affection which surrounded me. They had all become remote and unreal. Only our sun-drenched surroundings were real, and the glowing, happy faces of my three companions. My letters to the family must have been so inadequate and disappointing. They would expect much more from my imaginative pen than a copy-book description of a blue lake, a pine forest, and the towering peaks of the Jungfrau, Monch and Eiger. ('The monk is wearing his hat today, it's going to be fine!' Mark would tell us every morning on the sunny balcony, as we gazed at the distant peak, shrouded in a veil of mist.)

'Anyone would suppose Sarah had gone to Brighton, instead of the Bernese Oberland—the little she tells us!'—William would declare, perhaps with a hint of envy that I had so cleverly contrived to spend the summer in Switzerland, while he had remained fastened to a desk.

As the only English person for six weeks, in the Pension Gretelwald, I had received more than my share of attention, especially in the late evening, with the children in bed, and their mother quietly reading upstairs. I would be invited to dance, and drink beer, in the beer-garden. The dancing was fun, but the beer so distasteful I had to be served with coffee instead.

Joseph and Hans, both as sturdy and solid as oaks, together with their friends entertained their guests with national songs and dances. Then the three-piece band would crash suddenly into a foxtrot, and I would be clutched in the arms of Hans or Joseph, to canter around the small crowded tables. We were all amateurs in the dancing profession, so the one-step differed from the foxtrot only in *pace*—it was *faster!* The waltz was a great favourite with everyone, especially the elderly guests, and visitors from the village. 'The Blue Danube' was repeated at least six times every evening.

'Eenglish girls is vere nice. They dance goot,' my partners would insist politely, as we stumbled and stamped our way around the beer-garden. All this flattery, together with the affection of the children and their mother, had restored my self esteem. At last it seemed that I was finally and completely cured of shyness.

*   *   *   *   *

Finally the morning dawned when I woke to the unkind realisation that all our liberty and loitering must end. Papa Van de Goort was already on the way to collect us. The children were coaxed into silk blouses, white socks, and black patent shoes. Mathilde's hair had been washed and she had slept in curling rags. It was brushed into ringlets, and Mark's black hair shone with brilliantine.

Their mother appeared once again as an elegant and

sophisticated lady of society, in a new white ensemble, with a wide-brimmed hat, black gloves and shoes. She carried a parasol. I blinked and asked pertly,

'I suppose I have to dress up, too?'

She smiled a little wistfully, and patted my hand.

'To please me, Shearie, will you wear that rather nice little yellow dress—*and* your stockings.'

'To please *you*, I will even wear a hat and gloves!'

'Don't be naughty!' she warned, and added,

'Thank you, my dear, for your gay companionship. As for the children, I have never seen them happier with anyone.'

They were standing on the balcony now, waiting for their Papa. Tanned by the sun, to a golden brown, they were truly lovely, but already a little withdrawn from me.

'Thank you.' I could say no more without making a fool of myself, for tears pricked my eyes. This was the end of a short and sweet episode, that could never be repeated: next August the young French mademoiselle would take my place, for a holiday in Italy, and the following year, a German fraulein would join them for a holiday in Norway.

We were whisked away in Papa Van de Goort's purring limousine to a large, ostentatious hotel, in readiness for our 'grand tour' of the Bernese Oberland.

The waiter and the porter and the upstairs maid bowed and smiled deferentially, for Papa had booked an expensive suite, and we were obviously in the moneyed class! He propelled us through the restaurant to our reserved table at a panoramic window. The mountains, the lake, and the pine forest, seemed very remote indeed.

My single bedroom was lonely and isolated. I was 'Miss Shears' again, and very conscious of being a paid companion. We moved four times to luxury hotels, during the next two weeks, but the impression they left on my mind was as fleeting as shadows across a field of corn. Only the Pension Gretelwald was to remain in my memory. I could return there tomorrow and, I am convinced, find it unchanged—but for the fact that Joseph and Hans would be grandfathers!

*   *   *   *   *

Back at the English Church in The Hague, I sought my Dutch boy-friend, Willy, and found him happily installed in a pew, between two English nannies! Like Tom, at Victoria, he disliked 'being made use of', then dropped, for an indefinite period. And who could blame him? The nannies were more constant than I. It was a little disconcerting, though, to see them boarding the tram together, while I walked slowly around, alone.

'You cannot have your cake and eat it,' Mother would say. She was right. Mother was always right!

Without an escort, feeling independent and determined, I set off on one of my free days, soon after breakfast, in late September, with an urge to be really daring. Sheltered and protected in the comfortable residence of the Van de Goorts, I had to escape, to explore, to adventure—or lose my identity. Soon the summer season would close, and the little canal steamers put into dry dock for the winter. The coastal resort of Scheveningen would be bleak and dreary with closed shops and cafés and a deserted beach. The days would shorten, and soon I should be compelled to conform to the regular habits of the English nannies in The Hague on their free days —lunch in town, a cinema show, tea with cream cakes, and back to the house to spend the evening sociably or alone in the privacy of the bed-sitting room.

This programme had little appeal for me; I found it dull and I was a poor gossip. The English abroad, I had already noticed, seemed unimaginative, with a tendency to expect, even demand, English food. They could also be patronising to the 'foreigner' in his own country. Since all my free days before the summer holidays had been spent in the company of Willy and we had travelled around a great deal together, my early impressions of the English abroad had been bad, and on several occasions I was hot with shame and embarrassment, though Willy had seemed tolerant of such behaviour.

'You won't change their attitude when they have been encouraged since birth to consider themselves superior!' he laughed.

'Am I superior, Willy?'

'Yes, in a way.'

'I'm sorry—I don't mean to be.'

'Neither do they, it's inborn and part of the English character.'

'Who are the biggest offenders, from our three classes of society?'

'The middle class, quite definitely. I like what I've seen of your working class society, in my travels around London and the provinces, but we don't get many over here—only a few day-trippers to the bulb fields in May. Can't afford it, I suppose, with wages at a pretty low level for the average working class family. They go to Brighton and Blackpool for their holidays, as their parents did. As for the English gentry, they holiday abroad, but not on the other side of the Channel—maybe the South of France, Italy, Greece—but not Holland. There is nothing to attract them here, only diamonds and paintings, and even those would be bought by their agents.'

Willy was very well informed, and I had gleaned quite a lot of useful information in the few short weeks of our acquaintance. It was the lower middle class who apparently had the worst reputation for patronising the 'foreigner' and for insisting on English tea, English food, and 'English spoken' from the moment they stepped ashore. But Willy insisted it gave no offence, and I was exaggerating the embarrassment. The Dutch, he said, were a most hospitable people, and hospitality was not refused because their guests were a little difficult. Had I not noticed that porters, shop-assistants, waitresses, tram conductors, policemen, park keepers and so on, had all taken the trouble to learn a little English? Yes, I had.

*   *   *   *   *

The harbour at Rotterdam was a fascinating place, for ships from all over the world anchored there. It drew me back, like a magnet, that late September day. Seagulls screeched and dived for the scraps tossed through galley portholes. Strange tongues clamoured urgently on the decks, and cargo swung aloft. Old seafarers sat on the harbour wall, sucking on clay pipes. The strange voices, the screaming gulls, the clamour and clatter of the cargo, were music to their ears. They watched and listened, but said nothing. They were the only silent men, perhaps the only contented men, for they had had their day. Their homes, within a few feet of the harbour wall, housed their womenfolk. When the meal was ready they would go home, and come back, to sit on the harbour wall till dusk. Could any man ask more of life, at seventy? Their rugged faces revealed their contentment. Their blue searching eyes had not dimmed, and none wore spectacles.

I sat on the harbour wall a short distance away, and saw the same scene, but with different eyes, different thoughts. My thoughts had wings, my eyes strained to see beyond the harbour. Their voyages were over, but mine had scarcely started. That was the fundamental difference between us. The strange tongues, the smell of ships and sea, set alight in me this consuming desire to see, to feel, to know what lay beyond the horizon. It possessed me again, and tugged at my senses, this compelling urge to move on. Father had known it. Father would understand. If only he had lived.

A ferry boat was loading passengers on the quayside and I ran to jump aboard before it pulled away.

'Where are you going?' I asked in Dutch, for it was an easy and useful sentence. But the answer, to me, was unintelligible! That was the trouble, all the time, with elementary Dutch. I asked a question, but had no understanding of the answer.

The passengers stood quietly in a solid mass, quite unperturbed by the slight disturbance at the gangway. As the ferry shot forward, between the congested traffic of the harbour, I was thrilled and excited, at the unexpected adventure. And then I realised that most of the passengers were Chinese—not Dutch. Where were they going? It could only be a short distance, for the man at the quay had asked for only five cents. Smiling and clutching my hat in the freshening breeze, I looked around at my fellow passengers. Suddenly their faces split with wide grins, then shook with laughter. Two Chinese schoolboys, standing in the bows, pushed their way towards me. They too were laughing, but checked their laughter to say politely, in unison.

'Excuse me, please.' The elder boy went on breathlessly, 'we heard you ask where are we going, and we are very interested. It is very unusual to meet an English lady on the ferry. We should like to help you.'

'Thank you very much, but I'm really quite excited, and not at all nervous,' I assured them.

They looked a little puzzled, and the elder repeated, in perfect English,

'Excuse me, but it is very unusual. With your permission, we should like to escort you to my mother's house, for she is English. It is a Chinese settlement for seafaring people, and many hundreds have no work. My mother is the only English woman in the settlement. She was a stewardess, and she married my father who was a cook, twenty years ago,' he explained carefully. 'I have an English name, John, and this is my friend, Coca.'

Coca bowed, and agreed we should go to John's house.

'There is no danger, you understand, but it is a little unseemly for an English lady to walk alone through the streets,' he explained gravely.

The old-fashioned word 'unseemly' was strange on the tongue of a Chinese schoolboy. As the boat ground to a halt on the shingle, the boys jumped ashore, and each gave me a hand. John went on talking and explaining.

'It is a peninsular and we go to the city by train from the other side, but we use the ferry during the school term. We have many visitors and sightseers coming to have a look at us—like the animals in the zoo!' he laughed, as we clambered up the beach. 'But not the English visitors, perhaps they are not so curious, or not interested? My mother has not spoken to another English lady for a very long time. She will be so happy that I bring you!'

In his excitement, he hurried along, but my impressions of the place were disturbing, even a little frightening. I was glad of their company, for my vivid imagination could conjure up some very unpleasant and sinister characters from the inscrutable faces in the dark doorways, or the lean, hungry-looking figures propped against the walls.

(The memories of the Saturday film shows in the village hall were still much too vivid. The 'villian' of the piece had always been a cowboy with a gun, a Red Indian with a tomahawk, or a Chinaman with a stiletto! It would be years before I could associate a gentleman from China with anything but a stiletto.)

The deserted warehouses on the wharf, added to this alarming atmosphere of 'Limehouse', and I shivered, apprehensively, keeping close to the boys for protection. They hurried me through the dreary streets. It was damp and chill from waters of the harbour, surrounding the settlement on three sides, and the waters left behind a peculiar stagnant smell. A grey fog hung over this place, wrapping it in secrecy. The lounging idle figures in the doorways, and propped against the dingy walls, appeared for an instant, then vanished into the mist. I remembered, then, that the boy, John, walking beside me, had explained that the majority of these men had been out of work for years. They were 'paid off' cooks, stewards and deck hands—from the biggest ocean liners to the smallest tanker. Some had been 'signed on' by agents in the Far East, and for some reason or other, 'signed off' at Rotterdam.

John was still talking in a low-pitched voice, as we hurried past these huddled groups of men, in their silent, hopeless apathy. His own father, with a family of four children to support, had taken a job ashore, as a kitchen porter, in a hotel at Rotterdam. But for this privilege he had been charged a commission, which they could ill afford.

'Even so,' said John sensibly, 'it was better than waiting for hours in the agents' office, every week, only to be told there were no vacancies aboard-ship. He is a good man, my father,' he added respectfully.

Young Coca, who seemed to wait for the elder boy to take the lead, now took up the story of his own family.

'My father was a ship's steward, and he died of typhus in Singapore, when I was six years old. I have two brothers and a sister, and my mother works as a chamber-maid in a hotel. But soon I shall be fourteen years old and leaving school. Then I can start work as a bell-boy in this hotel. My mother has already arranged it,' he told me proudly.

'Coca is very ambitious, he plans to become a head waiter!' laughed his companion.

'And why not? Coca will make an excellent head waiter. But what are your own plans, John?' I asked.

'To go to College,' he answered without hesitation, and stared ahead, through the grey mist, into a future more bright and promising than his father's.

'John is the cleverest boy in the class, he will go to College,' Coca affirmed loyally.

'I am sure he will, there is always a way to realise an ambition, if you seriously want it.'

Then I told them about my own determination to travel, and its subsequent opportunity.

'Since I have no money, other than my wages, I must work my passage!' I laughed.

John's narrow black eyes shone like onyx in his pallid face.

'I have not met a lady who thinks this way. Always they wish to stay at home.'

Obviously, the boys were still puzzled, but we had found a common interest, in ambitions for the future.

* * * * *

'Mother! Mother! I have a lovely surprise for you!' called John from the bottom of a flight of dark stairs, leading to rooms over a small shop.

A thin grey-haired woman peered over the banisters, and I ran up to greet her. She grasped my two hands and asked incredulously,

'Where have you sprung from? Did you drop from the skies? Look who's here!' she called to her family, excitedly, as she pulled me in to a room crowded with furniture and screened in one corner, to make a kitchen. A round fat face beamed at me over the top of the screen.

'It's my husband, he is just off to work—shift-work,' she explained briefly. 'My two daughters come home to dinner, because they work in a factory only a short distance away—and this is my youngest son, Benny.'

Their smiles of welcome were warm and friendly, and the sense of being gathered into their midst, from the dreary world outside, was strangely comforting. Benny was a small replica of John. The girls had the grey eyes and fair skin of their mother. This was the first family of a mixed marriage I had ever met.

Apart from this one room, there appeared to be only one other, so how they arranged their sleeping accommodation, was a mystery. But the children were charming, well-mannered and well-dressed. Another wonderful mother, like mine, I thought, who was responsible for making a happy home in surroundings that would have defeated most women.

A place was quickly laid for me at the table, and a plate of chips, with a small meat ball, served first to me, as a guest, then to the family. They were wonderful listeners, and I talked incessantly! Benny was sent out to buy ice cream, then the mother made coffee, to complete the meal.

I was now in a new element—happy and excited as the family around me, for here, in this Chinese settlement, I had my first really appreciative audience. Anyone, who has anything to say, can be interesting and amusing, with an interested and amused audience.

At dusk, reluctant to leave, I had to start on the homeward journey, and the mother with her four children, escorted me to the tram, some distance away. From Rotterdam I caught a train back to The Hague, where I arrived much later than usual, so had to apologise and explain.

Papa Van de Goort was obviously very annoyed, and once again I was obliged to promise to refrain from such *dangerous escapades* in future.

To my everlasting regret I never saw the Chinese family again, after that day.

This incident may have hastened the arrival of the French mademoiselle, the following year, for my eighteen months' engagement was shortened to fifteen months. Very conscious of Papa Van de Goort's disapproval, from the start, I am sure he considered me a most *unsuitable* companion for his children. And he was probably right!

3

AT SEA

'I'll get you an introduction to one of the Directors of a shipping company in Glasgow,' said my Uncle Mac casually one day.

I looked at him in astonishment. He had married my favourite Aunt Emily but had scarcely noticed the existence of her nieces and nephews.

'You must always go straight to the top, when you want a job, Sarah. Subordinates are of no use to you at all,' he grinned disarmingly.

As a retired naval officer he was never far from the sea, and we had met by chance on the promenade, and decided to loiter for a while. Leaning back against a high breakwater he asked the question everyone had been asking for the past three months.

'Have you made any plans?'

'No, I hope something turns up soon, I'm getting desperate.'

'Your aunt tells me you've caught the travel bug?'

I nodded vigorously.

'A chip off the old block, eh? I never met your father, but he must have been quite a character.' Gazing with his far-reaching sailor's eyes at the English Channel, he went on, thoughtfully, 'Would you take a chance on board ship, as a member of the staff?'

'I'll take a chance on anything,' I told him emphatically.

It was then that he made the casual suggestion that set my course due East, for the next three years!

'Do you mean to tell me you actually *know* a Director of a shipping company?' I demanded.

'I know a lot of people, my girl, you would be surprised!'

He was ready to embark on a long tale of reminiscences, but I clutched his arm.

'Mac, if you can use your influence in any way I shall be eternally grateful.'

'For a Scotsman, it shouldn't present any difficulties at all,' he declared stoutly. 'No matter what his profession or rank a Scot will always see a fellow Scot as an equal. Did you know that? The Scottish educational system gives us that advantage, we all have equal opportunity. Mind you, it doesn't necessarily mean we all make good use of it later in life. That depends on the individual. But you will find a Scot at the top, more often than not, if you take the trouble to check on that statement—politics, banking, industry—I can think of quite a few big names from over the border, in these three spheres, for a start. As for shipping, well, I should say about fifty per cent of all shipping business in the United Kingdom is done in Glasgow.'

Allowing for a little natural exaggeration, I could appreciate his point.

'I'll write to Jock McKenzie. He's a pretty big noise. Went to school with him in Aberdeen, fifty years ago! I'll tell him he must find a job for my favourite niece on one of his passenger ships. Don't you worry, my girl—leave it to Mac!'

He kissed the tip of my nose, and went off to meet an old acquaintance for a drink, leaving me on the breakwater in a fever of eager anticipation. Could a childhood dream be realised this way? Could I work my passage to India? 'But what do you find beyond the horizon', I had demanded of William, some twenty years earlier. 'Is it the end of the world?' 'Of course not, stupid! It's the coast of France,' he told me knowledgeably.

* * * * *

I had to wait six months for the interview, following the introduction by letter. Mac had kept his word.

Mr McKenzie had written to me personally, explaining the system, rules and regulations of these staff appoointments. Vacancies were not advertised in the daily press, but filled only by recommendations. He continued;

'Since your uncle has informed me of your capabilities,

and your strong desire to travel, I shall be pleased to consider you for the next vacancy. To qualify for the post of children's stewardess, you will need no specific training, but common sense, adaptability, and possibly a sense of humour, would be useful.'

Well perhaps I had the last. Mrs Van de Goort had insisted that she recognised it that evening at Grosvenor House, yet I had not consciously been aware of it. As for the mixture of common sense, I had only to remember Mother's strict training, and everyone would consider me a most sensible person. Adaptability was an acquired asset. I had succeeded up to a point, with the Dutch family, but when that point was reached, and my independence crushed, I had to rebel. It was a risk I had to take.

The children in the care of the children's stewardess would normally be between the ages of two and ten, Mr McKenzie advised me. I had, therefore, to acquaint myself with two-year-olds before the interview, for I had completely forgotten how Henry and Jackie had behaved at that age. How *did* a two-year-old child behave? What did it eat? Could it take itself to the lavatory?

A family on leave from Malaya engaged me as a nurse for six weeks, and all these questions were soon answered. Indeed I began to doubt whether a sense of humour would survive the first week, if all two-year-olds behaved like the one from Malaya!

'Working my passage' was going to be no picnic. Children from the East, who have been left to native servants, are notoriously spoiled and unruly, I was told by an authority on such matters, when I confided my doubts.

'But you will only encounter such children on the home-ward journey. The outward voyage is paradise by comparison, and the children perfect angels. You will manage them beautifully!'

But had I the stamina and patience even for that short period? And would Mac have recommended me had he known I was liable to be sea-sick even before the ship sailed?

All these doubts vanished, as I met the twinkling grey eyes of the stout, balding man behind the big desk. His hand grasped mine firmly.

'So, you're Mac's niece, and you want to see the world?

Sit down, and we will see what we can do about it!' said Mr McKenzie, jovially.

In less than an hour I was out on the pavement, walking blissfully along in a drenching downpour. We were sailing from Liverpool early next month, and would be in Bombay for Easter.

*   *   *   *   *

The taxi slid to a halt on the wet quay at Liverpool, and I stepped out nervously. It was drab and deserted, on this grey February afternoon, and not at all the sort of place in which to linger. The driver apparently agreed with me for he also shivered, turned up the collar of his overcoat, and picked up my two heavy cases.

'I'll see you aboard, Miss. Docks is always a gloomy sort of place. Fair gives me the willies.'

My heart sank. The grey hulk of this unremarkable vessel on the quayside was a depressing sight.

'Come on then, follow me up this 'ere gangway, and mind yer step.'

'Up there?' I gasped—my head swimming dizzily at my first encounter with a narrow ladder.

Fixing my eyes on the downtrodden heels of his boots, I followed the driver, timidly, to the deck. A row of ten dark faces, with inquisitive black eyes, hung over the side.

''Ere you!' yelled my driver, irritably, dumping the cases on the wet slippery deck. 'Jump to it for Gawd's sake! Can't yer see the lady's arrived?'

They clustered around me, looked me up and down, found me extremely funny, and trembled with silent laughter. The driver swore and stamped with anger, but nothing could disturb their enjoyment of the situation. They were small and scraggy, with shrunken jackets, buttoned tightly across their thin chests.

'Thank you. I shall manage now, don't wait,' I told the angry driver. My knees were shaking and I was numb with cold and shock. 'Joining the ship at Liverpool' was so unlike anything I had imagined.

'What's going on here?' a gruff voice demanded, and a burly figure emerged in a crumpled suit, with a peaked cap pushed carelessly to the back of his head. He was unshaven, and his stubbly chin sank in the collar of a dark polo-neck jersey. His face was coarse, and his language coarser, as he addressed the group of coloured men and boys, whose grins had been wiped from their faces as with a wet sponge.

'Where the hell did you spring from?' he demanded—obviously shaken by my untimely arrival.

'I'm Sarah Shears, and I'm reporting for duty,' I informed him importantly.

Scratching his head, he also examined me carefully, from the crown of my modish little hat, to the toes of my new patent leather shoes.

'Didn't expect you till tomorrow,' he muttered, 'Pleased to meet you, Miss Shears. My name's Bates—Joe Bates—Chief Steward.'

He gripped my hand in a vice. What a scruffy-looking individual for a chief steward, I thought dispassionately, as he turned on the group once again.

'Well, come on Boy, what are you waiting for? Pick up the bags!'

One of the 'boys' sprang to attention, snatched up the heavy cases, and staggered away. We followed him down the companion-way.

'Guess you could do with a cup of tea?' said Joe Bates, surprisingly, over his shoulder.

Tea! My heart warmed towards him. I had, as usual, allowed my first impressions to influence me. Obviously Joe Bates was one of those 'rough diamonds' I had seen on the films but never met in real life.

The companion-ways were brightly lit with naked bulbs and the hot air quite suffocating after the cold deck. More coloured boys in striped cotton jackets and trousers were languidly cleaning the cabins. Our boy had stopped at a cabin door, in what Joe Bates described as 'mid-ships'.

'Dump the bags inside, Boy, then fetch some tea for the new mem-sahib,' he commanded.

'Yes, Boss,' answered the boy cheerfully, in a thin piping voice and vanished.

'That's *our* boy, Cleans our cabins, makes our beds, brings our tea—anything you like,' Joe Bates explained expansively.

'So we have a servant to wait on us and we in turn wait on the passengers?'

'That's how it goes,' he agreed, pushing open the door of a small crowded cabin, with a *double* bunk, but no porthole.

The only means of ventilation was through a glazed pane of glass in the ceiling. It was stuffy and stifling and stank of linament.

'Do I have to *share* a cabin?' I faltered.

''Fraid so—only heads of departments get a single cabin. You share with Mrs Bunce, the second stewardess. She's a good sort. Been going to sea for twenty years or more. You won't have no trouble with Annie Bunce.'

'I wasn't looking for trouble, Mr Bates. But I did expect a cabin to myself.'

'Sorry about that—call me Joe,' he invited, slapping his chest.

If I suffered from claustrophobia, as well as sea-sickness, I should be in a sorry state of health by the time we reached Bombay, I was thinking, desperately, when the boy slid through the door with a tray of tea. I could see now that his hair was grey at the temples, and his thin hands wrinkled. His gliding movements were soft and swift as a cat's, and his eyes too big for his shrunken face.

'Thank you, Boy,' I smiled, and he returned the smile, shyly, with the slightest little bow.

'It is a pleasure, Mem-sahib.' He slid away noiselessly.

There were two tea cups on the tray, large and thick-rimmed, and some biscuits on a plate. Joe pushed aside a pile of scattered clothes, and sat down, uninvited on the lower bunk. Then he poured the tea.

'Expect Mrs Bunce has gone to the flicks with Mrs Hammond. They go most afternoons, the week before sailing,' he told me.

'Is Mrs Hammond the Chief Stewardess?'

He nodded, sipping the hot, strong tea, with noisy relish.

'What's she like, Joe?'

'Not bad—bit of a madam. I'm not one of her blue-eyed boys!' he chortled. 'She's dead keen on the First Mate, but he happens to be a confirmed bachelor.'

'Hasn't she got a husband, then?'

'Widow, and Annie Bunce, both widows. Lost their husbands in the war. Both Merchant Navy men. Funny sort of life for women, no settled home, and not much comfort—still they seem to like it.'

He picked up a grubby blouse, stained and sour with sweat, and searched my face.

'This sort of thing, now—don't take no notice. You'll soon get used to it. Poor old Annie, she sweats like a pig in the Tropics!'

I shuddered and sipped my tea. The shelf of the tiny dressing-table was white with face powder, and a dark rim stained the small wash-basin. The cabin was cluttered with shoes and discarded clothes. Only the top bunk—my bunk—was neat and tidy, with clean sheets and blankets.

'She seems to have left in a hurry,' I commented dryly, my head throbbing with tiredness and the unaccustomed disorder and heat of the cabin.

'It's always like this—I never seen it any other way,' said Joe.

'Tell me about the rest of the crew.'

'You mean *staff*,' he corrected. 'That's our department. Well, there's the Purser—your immediate boss, by the way, then myself, as Chief Steward, with two young assistants, and a bunch of lazy cabin boys, all coloured. Then two stewardesses, six Indian waiters, and, of course, the Chef, and his gang in the galley.

'Now the crew consists of First, Second, Third and Fourth Mate, three young Quarter-Masters, seven Engineers—all Scots—and those dark fellows, you saw on deck—Lascars from Calcutta. We also have a carpenter, known as 'Chips', two wireless operators, known as 'Old Sparks' and 'Young Sparks', and a doctor who joins the ship on sailing day with the passengers.'

I gaped. It seemed a surprising number of people for a tourist class passenger ship of very moderate proportions.

'The Old Man is a stickler for routine and discipline. Inspection every morning, so watch out!'

'The Old Man?'

He grinned. 'The *Captain*—and he's a woman-hater!'

'I'm scared to death, honestly Joe. It sounds too much like a floating hotel, with all these heads of departments, and grades of service.'

'You're telling me, young woman. Once you've signed on

the dotted line you're as much a prisoner as if you was shut up in Brixton Jail! It's a contract, see, and you're a blinking servant of the Company and the passengers, till you sign off again at Liverpool. Strict! I'll say it's strict. But don't you worry, my girl. There are compensations in plenty, once we get ashore at Bombay!' He winked. 'You'll have the time of your young life, I shouldn't wonder. Well, I must get along and check up on those lazy little bastards! Cheerio! See you later!'

After Joe had left, I slipped off my new shoes, and climbed up to the top bunk. Stretched on a grey army blanket, I closed my eyes on the general disorder, but the varous odours, a mixture of linament, cheap face powder, and sweat, still disturbed me.

My sense of smell was certainly the most acute of all my senses, for I remembered all the places I had seen and known by a certain peculiar smell attached to the place. With my eyes closed I could travel back to the hop-gardens of Kent, to the freshness of the first primroses in Spring, the acrid smell of sulphur on Mother's stained hands as she handed out the slabs of cold bread pudding, the sickly smell of Syrup of Figs in the spoon held under my nose.

The old nostalgia gripped me, and my eyes were wet under their closed lids. Oh, this intolerable homesickness! It was the penalty of independence, to be paid in such moments of loneliness and isolation. I couldn't convince myself at such bleak moments that I really wanted to adventure, for I was too vulnerable.

What had persuaded me to pack my bags again, to take the train to Liverpool—to 'join the ship' in dock, together with this motley crowd of strangers and a casual room-mate who hadn't even bothered to welcome me? I must be more than a little mad! This stuffy, untidy cabin was no substutite for home. Bombay was a mirage—just one of the lovely names I had found so fascinating. Bombay . . . Benares . . . Baghdad . . . Bangalore. Now in this dreary compartment they held no more fascination than Brighton or Blackpool!

*   *   *   *   *

'You asleep?'

I opened my eyes and looked down on the homely face and

plump little figure of Annie Bunce. My watch showed me I had slept for nearly two hours!

'It's pelting cats and dogs, but we managed to get a taxi,' she shook the raindrops from a faded felt hat, and tossed it on the lower bunk, then dropped her coat on the floor. Her panting bosom was enfolded in a tight woolly jumper, and the seams of the dark skirt near to bursting, as she bent over to unlace her shoes.

'I see you've had some tea? I could do with a cup myself.'

She opened the door and yelled—'Boy!'—in a voice that rattled the empty tea cups.

He appeared, in answer to her summons, calm and unperturbed, with his shy, deferential smile,

'Yes, Mem-sahib?'

'Tea, Boy!—and make some ham sandwiches, I'm starving! Bring enough for the new mem-sahib and don't be half the night about it!'

His face was empty of all expression now, and I wondered what he felt beneath that serene countenance. Did he realise that his British 'superiors' were working class employees of the shipping company? Why were these 'boys' so despised? From the moment I set foot on the deck and the taxi driver bellowed 'Here, you!', this despicable rudeness had been more noticeable than any other factor. Joe Bates was obviously a bully, and now Annie Bunce was treating herself to the same loud superiority. They were Lascars from Calcutta—Joe Bates had explained, as though they had no status at all, no individuality. What exactly *was* a Lascar—a class, or a nationality?

*   *   *   *   *

There seemed no room for me down below, so I stayed on my bunk, awaiting the second tray of tea, while Annie Bunce pulled on a pair of comfortable slippers, and pushed a few hair pins into the loose strands of grey hair. Her face was pallid from long years of confined space and poor ventilation, but her eyes as bright as amber beads. She was the most casual person I had ever met, and took no more notice of me than the old hat she had tossed aside. Evidently human relationships did not trouble her.

But where was Mrs Hammond?

She arrived in answer to my unspoken question, in the

doorway, followed by Boy, with a loaded tray. I hurriedly swung my legs over the side and dropped to the floor, to greet her, for she was, after all, my superior officer. We shook hands cordially.

'Mr Bates informed me you had arrived, but you were not expected today,' she reminded me.

She was tall and slim, and her tailored costume fitted perfectly. But her grey eyes held no warmth, and her mouth drooped in a disagreeable way.

'I told Boy to bring my tea in here. No, I won't eat anything, it's too near supper time, and I have to study my figure!'

Anne Bunce chuckled, and seized a sandwich, pouring tea at the same time. Mrs Hammond sat down on the small bench against the wall, which served as a chair, and they chatted about the film they had seen. I waited, politely, for Mrs Hammond's attention, for I was anxious to know about my duties and my uniform. At last they were finished with Spencer Tracey and Bette Davis.

'I hope you are a good sailor, for we shall both be fully occupied for the first ten days or so, looking after our sea-sick passengers. So don't count on us for any support,' Mrs Hammond began. 'The children will be your responsibility whenever their mothers decide to abandon them, between the hours of 7 am and 6 pm—seven days a week.'

Then she asked me bluntly if I had fully realised the dangers to which children could be subjected on board ship?

No, I hadn't. So she listed them at enormous and horrifying length. I felt my shoulders sagging under the weight of so much responsibility.

'What you really need, of course, is a second pair of eyes—in the back of your head!' Mrs Hammond reminded me, with a lady-like titter of amusement, as she sipped the third cup of tea.

*   *   *   *   *

The 'skeleton staff' gathered for supper in the dining saloon, with two of the boys to wait on their demands. Joe Bates had shaved and brushed his hair, and I met the Chef—a Pickwickian character, with an enormous stomach, and short legs. He seemed to delight in teasing Annie Bunce, but she was a good match for him.

'Not much choice on the menu tonight, Sarah. We have to make do in port, but you wait till dinner on sailing day, my girl, and you won't know whether you're staying at the Ritz or Savoy!'

His wheezy laugh rattled in his chest, and his face had the same unhealthy pallor as the rest of the seniors at the table. But his 'making do' amused me. We had onion soup, lamb cutlets (Joe Bates and Annie Bunce ate three apiece) a variety of vegetables, lemon meringue pie, cheese and biscuits and coffee.

It was a leisurely meal, and Joe handed round a packet of cigarettes as soon as he had finished his second helping of pie. The Purser, 'Old Sparks' and the Third Mate, dined in solitary isolation at another table, removed from the rabble. I was introduced, but they were deep in earnest conversation.

The Purser's cursory glance was not reassuring. He looked displeased over some matter or other, and spoke with the sharp authority of one accustomed to giving orders.

The Second Engineer—a tremendous man with a quiet voice, and gentle manner—joined us at our table for supper, together with 'Chips' a wizened little man with a drooping moustache.

The youngest engineer, freckle-faced, and very much a novice, like myself, sat silent throughout the meal. We both refused a cigarette, and sat quietly listening to our elders exchanging the day's gossip and grumbles.

The Chef who had eaten less than anyone, was drinking black coffee, and Joe Bates was collecting the money for the football sweep. He left the table, inviting the Chef and the 'Second' to join him for a game of poker later in the evening. His language was as coarse as his appearance and yet I felt a definite liking for this man. He had been the first to greet me, and offer me tea, and even if the clumsy welcome lacked warmth, it was typical of him.

As for the Purser, my immediate boss—I was going to dislike him intensely!

Wandering round on a tour of inspection, after supper, I thought I had never seen a more dreary place. Then I saw the boys disappearing below, to the well deck, where, I imagined, they would be eating their own kind of food, talking their own language, and behaving like normal human beings. As I stood there, looking down into the murky darkness, lit only by a solitary naked bulb, a shout of laughter reached me, and I smiled with relief and pleasure.

So, clutching at the last shreds of the obligatory 'sense of humour', I went back to enquire on the nature of the new uniform I had been instructed to buy at a big departmental store in Liverpool the following day. I was surprised and delighted to discover I should be wearing navy blue serge, with brass buttons, and a most becoming nursing sister's cap of white starched muslin, in home waters. I should change, with the rest of the staff, and officers, into an all-white uniform, in that part of the world known vaguely as 'the Tropics'.

My spirits soared rapidly at such a pleasing prospect, and I climbed happily to the top bunk, with my copy of *Jane Eyre*.

* * * * *

I had 'signed on', received my first pay, and allocated half my wages to Mother (she saved every penny, and returned it to me during a period of unemployment, three years later).

'Have you any dependents?' asked the shipping clerk automatically, without even glancing up from the document under his thumb.

Since the six previous 'recruits' had replied in the affirmative, I did the same.

'Mother.'

'Address?'

He scribbled busily, then nodded abruptly, and passed on to the next.

Mother will be surprised, I thought, at such a sudden burst of generosity, for I had often to borrow money.

* * * * *

Now every companion-way echoed to the clatter of boots, cranes and crates swung aloft, and orders were shouted. Men cursed each other heartily from dawn till dusk. The noise was deafening. I was told that all would be ship-shape by Saturday —only three days away.

Meals were hurried, tempers frayed, and I was constantly hustled out of the way, or instructed to take a pile of sheets to the cabin for patching. Boy slid in and out with trays of tea and sandwiches; an anxious frown puckering his eyes. 'Yes, Mem-sahib, no, Mem-sahib,' he answered mechanically, listening for the harsh voice of Joe Bates, who was rampaging round the cabins like an enraged bull, and threatening to murder all the 'lazy little bastards'.

The engineers—all six of them—emerged from the engine room in oily dungarees, followed by the 'Chief'—a dour Scot, with a reputation for efficiency.

'Young Sparks', flicking dust from an immaculate grey suit, dashed about the boat deck, with a collection of gadgets, wireless sets and musical instruments, with which he intended to amuse himself when off duty. A bit of a dandy, with blond hair, he also brought a good supply of shirts for 'the Tropics', and a dinner jacket, since he expected to be invited to dine out at the swankiest hotel in Bombay. This was his second voyage, so he was well acquainted with his duties, not too arduous, and had already acquired a few influential friends.

'Old Sparks' was highly amused by the antics of his junior, and paced up and down his small domain, smoking a pipe, and apparently quite unaffected by all the disturbance down below. I took one look at his kind, pleasant face, and decided he was the only person in whom I could confide, in any real trouble.

Whenever I managed to escape from the patching of sheets, and the gossip of the stewardesses, I fled to the boat deck, to find 'Old Sparks' in his tiny cabin, preparing for the voyage with quiet ease. Grey-haired and fiftyish, calm and unruffled, he was the perfect father figure, to admire and respect. He always greeted me with the same question,

'Well, my dear, and how have they been treating you today?'

And after listening sympathetically, would proceed to give me some good advice.

'I'm not so sure that you haven't made a mistake,' he began dubiously, the night before the passengers came aboard. 'You know, Sarah, you are a bit of a rebel, and you won't take kindly to all the strict rules and regulations enforced on every member of the staff and crew, from the moment we leave this dock. It's a little world, afloat on the ocean for twenty-five days, and as far removed from the rest as the stars in the sky—apart from the few hours in dock at Marseilles and Port Said—and that won't concern you because you won't be allowed to go ashore.'

'But why not?' I protested. 'I was looking forward to that experience.'

'Just one of those rules and regulations I was telling you about,' he continued. 'This first voyage is not only an experience of a rather unusual nature, for a young woman like yourself, but also a lesson in self-discipline. You must, up to a point, conform to the pattern, Sarah. A high standard of behaviour is expected, but don't, for heaven's sake, lose your enjoyment of this first voyage. It can never be repeated, my dear—the novelty, the wonder, the beauty and splendour, can never be repeated or forgotten as long as you live. After a few days you will feel as far removed from your family and friends as though they lived on another planet. It's quite extraordinary. Are you a good sailor?'

'No, rotten!'

'Oh, you poor child. Keep it dark till we embark!'

His eyes twinkled behind a cloud of smoke, as he relit the pipe.

'As Joe Bates would say "You've got a bloody nerve!" ' he chortled.

*   *   *   *   *

When I opened my eyes at six o'clock that Saturday morning, Boy was already holding out two cups of tea, calling softly, but persistently,

'Mem-sahib. Mem-sahib.'

Annie Bunce rolled over heavily and I bounced on my bunk overhead.

'What's the time?' she mumbled irritably.

'Six o'clock, Mem-sahib. Passengers soon be here!' said Boy, brightly, in his thin, piping voice.

'Oh, Lord! I had forgotten.'

She sat up and Boy handed her the tea, then passed mine over her head. He was well trained and extremely diplomatic, I had noticed during the week, and now he had already served Mrs Hammond with early tea, then Annie Bunce, and last of all, myself, as the youngest and newest stewardess. But the dark face, tilted backwards, as he handed up the cup and saucer, held the kind of benevolence of an ayah, smoothing the path of her charges.

'Fine day, Mem-sahib. No rain!' he told me soothingly.

'Oh buzz off, Boy, I want to get dressed.'

Annie Bunce could swallow a cup of scalding hot tea

quicker than anyone else. For her size, she was amazingly nimble, and years of stewarding had taught her the quickest way to wash and dress, prepare a tray, and serve it.

'I go, Mem-sahib,' said Boy obediently, but she was already on her feet, padding about in a tight flannelette nightdress.

Plunging her face into the wash-basin, she gurgled,

'Shan't be two shakes of a lamb's tail, so stay where you are. From to-morrow, I must be up at five-thirty. Heaven knows how many oranges to squeeze. The kids have orange juice, as well as all the trays of tea for all my passengers. Got to keep to a tight schedule now, and we have to be finished by seven-thirty.'

She dropped her nightdress to her waist, vigorously sponged her armpits, and went on talking, for she never stopped from the moment she set her feet on the cabin floor. Her underwear consisted of two garments, knickers and petticoat, and the clean uniform dress, with its brass buttons, slid over her head. In a matter of seconds she had rolled on her black stockings and laced her shoes. Twisting her hair into a knot, she filled her mouth with hair-pins, then jammed them carelessly into her head. The starched muslin cap hid all the defects, pulled well down on her smooth brow, leaving her pallid face exposed and shining. But the bright eyes gave her plain features a young and lively appearance. With the uniform dress she had slipped on a new personality. The slackness and sloppiness belonged, apparently, in dock, together with the old slippers, the shabby skirt and tight woolly jumpers.

'Shan't see much of you today, too busy. All on our toes, you bet! Well, so long. Watch out for the kids, can't trust 'em! And don't forget your cap. Old Herb will have a fit if he catches you without it.'

She bounced through the door, and I slid to the floor. Herb? Did she mean the Purser, Herbert Lowry? I reminded myself of the good advice 'Sparks' had given me about behaviour. 'From the moment you leave this dock, you are on duty, and in the public eye'. The week had been long, tedious and confusing. I was glad to be starting on a definite routine, for now, suddenly, everything was ship-shape and ready for sailing.

The decks were scrubbed, the brasses gleamed, clean curtains draped the polished windows. Immaculate white linen covered the tables in the dining saloon, and huge bouquets of flowers decorated the lounge. Going on duty for the first time in my new uniform I walked briskly and proudly down the companion-way. My shipmates greeted me with fresh interest and backward glances.

All were dressed in navy blue serge, with brass buttons, and caps at exactly the right angle. The transformation was quite extraordinary, and Joe Bates was quite good-looking in a rugged sort of way!

The ship's officers—undeniably handsome—strode past like lords of creation. The Chef was wearing the tallest hat I had ever seen, and a spotless white coat. The boys in clean striped trousers and white jackets, stood to attention at cabin doorways, or grouped together at strategic points, ready to handle the luggage. And most magnificent of all, six figures in turbans and white robes sashed with blue, were waiting to serve early breakfast to the first arrivals.

It was strangely thrilling and exciting. It was like the opening night of a new play, with all the cast assembled on the stage, and the same nervous tension prevailing. I was one of the cast, and had learned my lines. They hung in my mind like a string of beads.

'The children are your responsibility whenever the mothers decide to abandon them. You will be on duty from 7 a.m. till 6 p.m.—seven days a week. Had you realised the dangers to which children can be subjected on board ship? Apart from falling overboard, crashing head first down campanion-ways, breaking limbs on slippery decks, and drowning in the swimming pool, there was also the danger of choking over a fish-bone, or being scalded with hot soup. They must be watched and supervised, cosseted and coddled. Tears and tantrums should be instantly pacified. Ice cream, sweets and biscuits to be used lavishly, regardless of cost. The children must be kept occupied, happy and contented, twelve hours a day, for twenty-five days.'

I was word perfect!

'Get your breakfast, the first family are not due for an hour,' snapped the Purser, from his office doorway.

His eyes were cold as steel as they travelled over my small neat figure, but he was totally impartial.

'Thank you, Mr Lowry.'

Did he expect to be addressed as 'Sir' by a junior stewardess?

I joined the Chef at the staff table, and we breakfasted together.

'You look very cheeky this morning, my girl,' he winked expansively.

We waited for our bacon and eggs in a comfortable silence; watched by the tall impassive, turbaned waiter.

The curtain was up!

*　　*　　*　　*　　*

Fortified by a good substantial breakfast, and the Chef's appreciation of my company, I stood ready for the first onslaught in a conspicuous position on the companion-way.

I hadn't long to wait.

Two noisy little boys, followed by a young, distraught mother with a toddler, raced up the gangway, and plunged in through the wide open door. They ran the length of the companion-way whooping excitedly, watched by a group of grinning 'boys'. Mrs Hammond and the Purser, both wearing the fixed smiles that stuck to their faces all day, stood waiting to catch the children at the far end. The boys stopped abruptly, stared at the uniformed figures and bolted back to their mother.

I hovered in the background, lest she decide to abandon them to my care immediately. Escorted by Mrs Hammond and a steward staggering under a load of so-called 'hand luggage', they all tumbled into Cabin 27. Shrieks of joy reached me as the boys bounced on all the bunks in turn, while the toddler yelled for attention.

All through the long morning families arrived, and I continued to hover. But none of the younger children had any intention of losing sight of their mother, and clung tenaciously to her skirt, or hung on her neck with throttling arms. They were shy, sullen or sad, according to their moods, or the extent of their tiredness. Some had been travelling all night, and were drooping with sleep; several sat down on the deck and had to be picked up and carried to their cabins, screaming and kicking. Only the two little boys, fresh as the morning dew, continued to race madly up and down, tripping up unsuspecting toddlers, and colliding with stewards laden with luggage. I followed their movements anxiously, but they ignored me completely.

'Would you like to see the nursery? We have a lovely new rocking horse and lots of toys,' I called after them, but they ran on unheeding.

'They are just letting off steam!' their mother explained fondly, from the cabin door.

All my shipmates seemed to be tearing around on their own urgent business, and I caught a glimpse of Annie Bunce, with a sleeping baby draped over one shoulder, leading a child by the hand. She seemed to have the right approach, I thought enviously, but her long experience would have given her that advantage over me. While I hesitated, she dashed forward, snatching babies and bundles from their mother's arms. Her eyes were bright with welcome, and she seemed to be enjoying every moment.

'You've seen nothing yet, my girl—you wait till the boat train arrives! That really is pandemonium!' she warned me boisterously.

'But I've done nothing but hang around all morning,' I complained.

'Never you mind, your turn will come. With all these kids swarming over the place you won't know whether you are coming or going. Nearly forty this trip, but quite a few infants, and several families with their own nannies, so that's a few less for you to worry about.'

She swallowed three sandwiches and two cups of tea in a matter of seconds, and was ready for the fray.

'Keep an eye on the dining saloon—meals laid on practically all day. You might be needed to give a hand with feeding the tots. Just dashing off now to make up a couple of bottles for the infants. Sick all over the place, poor little blighters,' she chortled happily, as she bustled away. This was a new Annie Bunce today, and I hardly recognised her as the same woman.

'Pandemonium' was the right word! It was the most confusing and distracting day I had ever known. 'On duty' but without a single duty to perform, I was swept aside in the scramble for cabins and refreshments. Anxious mothers dragged their tired and bewildered offspring by the hand, and clamoured for attention.

'Stewardess! I'm dying for a cup of tea, will you attend to it?' drawled a haughty platinum blonde.

'I'm so sorry. Will you ring for your steward, please. I'm the children's stewardess,' I informed her brightly.

'Oh really? Well, as it happens I haven't any.'

Her husband looked over her shoulder and inspected me closely.

'Children's stewardess, eh? Well, keep the little blighters under control. Need a firm hand. Never seen so many at this time of the year. Should have booked on the 'P & O' I suppose. Can't trust these tourist class vessels. Come on, darling, let's find the bar. We need something stronger than tea!'

I watched them walk away, and I was very thankful they had no children to abandon to my care. They would probably have behaved like their parents.

My new nursery was still deserted, so I wandered out on deck to get a breath of fresh air. 'Old Sparks' hung over the rail of the boat deck, still smoking his pipe, still calm and unperturbed by all the disturbance. He waved his pipe and called out cheerily.

'How's it going?'

I shrugged and spread my hands in a gesture of resignation, for it was a long, boring day.

'Only another four hours to sailing, if we are dead on schedule.'

He shouted against the din of loading and unloading, and the clatter of trucks and lorries on the quay. It was bedlam everywhere, inside and out and only 'Sparks' seemed to have escaped, in his private little world on the boat deck. But suddenly even he was disturbed by the yapping of several dogs.

'Here they come! Got the kennels up here,' he called down to me.

'Kennels? Did you say kennels?' I yelled back. 'Are we taking dogs to India?'

He cupped his hands to his mouth. 'Good luck! see you in Bombay!'

In the open doorway the Purser's disapproving face hit me like a douche of cold water. He stepped backwards as I slipped past, and our eyes met in mutual dislike. He was determined to keep me subordinate, but I was equally determined now to keep a small measure of independence—or I might as well have stayed in Brighton!

Staff dinner was served at six-thirty. As I sat down to a generous helping of roast turkey, I felt the ship move and shudder, and a throbbing vibration all about me. It was a most extraordinary sensation—exciting yet also a little frightening.

Across the table, Joe Bates caught my eye, and grinned.

'We're on our way. Next stop Marseilles!'

He passed me the gravy with a broad wink. I did not sit down at that table again for five days!

*   *   *   *   *

It was all a question of mind over matter, I had read in a magazine article. Your brain cells told your body exactly what to do and how to behave. It was as simple as that. But even before I had finished the trifle I had grave doubts of its feasibility. The throbbing and shuddering of the ship was real, not imaginary. I saw it as a gigantic monster, stretching, after a long sleep. Its throbbing heart was down below, in the engine room. It was a female monster, existing only for her own pleasure, hurrying towards the sea.

'She's a bit unsteady tonight,' I heard someone say as I left the table.

'She never cares much for the river, anyway,' 'Chips' declared knowledgeably, helping himself to a chunk of Gorgonzola cheese.

The walls closed in as I walked drunkenly down the corridor. Everything was alive, swaying and sliding dizzily. My eyes could not focus properly. All about me was disturbing motion and movement. It must be an illusion, of course, I reminded myself, when we were still in the river, and not yet on the open sea? It was just a question of mind over matter, and all I had to do was reach the cabin, lie down quietly and it would pass!

Knowing that my services were no longer required and breathing a fervent prayer of thanks to a rather remote God, I clutched my heaving stomach and staggered to the nearest bathroom.

'You look a bit green, Nurse, feeling all right?' The husband of the haughty blonde, stepping briskly down the corridor, had collided with me.

Ashamed and humiliated, I faltered,

'Yes, thank you, I'm fine.'

He puffed a cloud of cigar smoke over my throbbing head, and went on his way to the bar. I could imagine him cracking some good jokes about a stewardess who was sea-sick before we even got to the sea!

The stuffy little cabin had never seemed so cosy, for I was shivering uncontrollably now. Annie Bunce was still busy settling her passengers and had not had dinner. She would bring it down to the cabin on a tray, later, when she had finished her duties, she had informed me carelessly. She would often have to take her breakfast and dinner on a tray, during the first week of the voyage, when more and more passengers took to their bunks.

'I'm used to it—eat anything, any time. Can't work on an empty stomach, though—stands to reason.'

Stretched on the top bunk, I closed my eyes and pretended sleep, when the door burst open some time later. A strong whiff of sausages, bacon, Brussels sprouts and gravy, wafted up to me, as she lifted the cover.

'Smells good! Chef gave me a double helping of turkey. Said I deserved it,' I heard her say.

Reaching for my dressing-gown, I slid off the bunk and disappeared. When I returned some time later, she was scooping up a large mound of strawberry ice cream, and the smell of the roast dinner was disguised now by the more pungent smell of freshly brewed coffee. She offered me a cup.

'No, thanks.'

I climbed back carefully, and wrapped the blankets round my shivering body. My stomach ached unbearably.

'You all right?' Annie Bunce demanded.

'Just a headache,' I lied.

'Yes, it's a bit of a nightmare, for a newcomer. Get this day over and the rest is plain sailing,' she told me.

Kicking off her shoes, she leaned back comfortably to light a cigarette. She was not a heavy smoker, but even that innocent little cloud drifting over my head was nauseating.

My throat tightened with the pain of defeat and desolation.

'You're a fine one!' grumbled Annie Bunce early the next morning, when I had stepped over her so many times we were both dizzy. 'Sick already in this bit of a swell, whatever will you be like in the Bay?'

'Which Bay?' I faltered.

'Bay o' Biscay—she rolls and tosses like a mad thing in these spring tides. Everything battened down and all the portholes locked. Gives me an appetite, I eat like a horse in the Bay!'

She chuckled. 'Now take my advice, my girl, and eat a good breakfast, can't work on an empty stomach.'

Then she rolled over, closed her eyes and began to snore lustily.

'Tea, Mem-sahib.'

Boy's soft voice brought the long night to an end.

'No, thank you.'

'Mem-sahib sick?'

I nodded mutely.

Annie Bunce drank both cups of tea that morning, and five subsequent mornings, for Boy was patient and persistent.

'I bring you orange juice, or lemon. Yes?'

'Nothing, thank you.'

He was quite distressed, and his warm sympathy compensated for the jeers and sarcasm of my shipmates. A sea-sick stewardess was not only a nuisance (for someone had to mind the kids when she galloped off to the bathroom, as Annie Bunce pointed out quite reasonably) but also an embarrassment to the Purser, who had to report everything to the 'Old Man'. With Mr McKenzie's personal recommendation they had all expected a good sailor. All the hearty individuals who marched around the deck ten times before dinner invited me to join them.

'You do look funny,' said one small girl who had been swaying back and forth on the rocking horse for a full twenty minutes.

It was our third day at sea, and only three children remained in my care, completely abandoned by sea-sick mothers. They were as lively and boisterous as ever, demanding all my attention and all my patience. Meal times were a nightmare.

In the swaying dining saloon, three magnificent waiters hovered behind the children's chairs while they decided what they would eat. My tentative suggestions were ignored, and I was too ill to argue. The four-year-old ate nothing but sausages, three times a day, and lashings of chocolate ice cream. A tiny girl of three, who looked so frail I was terrified to lose sight of her, demanded 'Chips, more chips', imperiously, and one of the turbaned waiters would hurry away, shrugging his handsome shoulders resignedly. Such items as porridge, breakfast cereal, bread and butter, and milk pudding were completely rejected. But grapefruit, mushrooms, lemon meringue pie and pancakes, were firm favourites, together with sausages, chips and ice cream.

The savoury smells from the serving hatch played disastrous tricks on my sick stomach, and I draped myself around a door-post, ready to dash away.

'What you need, my girl, is a breath of fresh air, you look like death warmed up,' said Joe Bates that evening, as the three children were led away to be bathed and put to bed by Annie Bunce.

Poor Mrs Hammond with all her families confined to their cabins, staggered round the corridors with trays of refreshments and jugs of lemon barley water.

Empty and limp as a pricked balloon, I stood leaning back against the bulkhead on the aftdeck, clutching it fearfully with both hands. The grey sea rolled in mountainous waves, and the ship rose and slid down, shuddering on each successive wave. Appalled, yet strangely fascinated, I could not move away.

I had dragged the cap from my aching head, and though wrapped in an overcoat, over my uniform dress, I was still shivering wretchedly and longed to die. The wind tossed and tangled my hair over my face, but I was too terrified to push it out of my eyes.

In a split second of its parting, I glanced up and met the dark, searching eyes of the Third Mate. He was muffled in oilskins, and just going on watch. Tall, frowning, but incredibly handsome, he stood there, revelling in the gale.

I stared, and he stared back, unsmiling.

Then he swung round, leaped down the companion-way, unclasped my clutching fingers, gave my shoulders an encouraging squeeze and pushed me inside.

Not a word was spoken between us, but I adored him, then and there.

Climbing dizzily up to my bunk that evening, I took a sheet of paper and a pencil and wrote:

Winter Voyage

When February's gloom and strange peculiar smells my senses
    stirred,
When all around the chill of faces new, noises, and scattered
    chaff was poured,

When from the cabins' dim interior moaned the sirens of the
   ships on way,
And figures darting through the mist were lost,
I found my way.
Behind a wall of faces raised to criticise my youth,
And voices seeming harsh in jokes uncouth,
Two eyes looked down, that neither jeered, nor found in me a
   thing to be despised,
But pierced the faltering courage of a novice,
Bound at Fortune's wheel when chance arise,
You came from whence the breezes blow across the Weald,
And men are free to cast their shadows in a field,
All this I knew, yet you had not spoken,
But never shall the spell you wove be broken.

*   *   *   *   *

'What's this I hear about the Children's Stewardess not
reporting for staff meals for the past five days?' demanded the
ship's doctor, testily.

I was putting away scattered toys and picking up toffee
papers, prior to going off duty. Increasingly vulnerable, I
burst into tears.

'Oh, shucks! I didn't mean it unkindly. Sit down, my dear,
and let's have a look at you.' He felt my pulse and went on
talking. 'Have you tried to eat anything?'

'Yes, but it's no use!' I wailed. 'I get sicker and sicker.'

He was young and inexperienced, but terribly self-possessed.

'It has been a pretty rough passage,' he agreed. 'Some of my
patients have been really ill, but the worst is over, so cheer up!
I'll put you on Allenbury's Baby Food for a couple of days. It
will make a good lining for that queezy stomach of yours. Then
you go on to a light diet of steamed fish and chicken—understand?'

'Yes, doctor,' I sniffed humbly.

He patted my hand, promised me a whale of a time in the
Mediterranean, and sauntered away. Several days later he
returned, hot, flustered, and not in the least self-possessed.

'That damn woman! She must have known that child
Deidre had a rash,' he stormed, 'wretched child has developed
measles!'

I was struck dumb, and so were the twenty children playing
in the nursery.

'Has she been here?' he demanded.

'Practically all day.'

He groaned, and paced up and down between the two play-pens holding my four youngest charges.

'Ever had measles yourself, nurse?'

'I expect so, I had most things as a child.'

'Well, we are in for a pretty grim period, the two of us.'

Swelling with pride and self-importance, I told him,

'I'm ready, doctor. Just tell me what I have to do.'

He ruffled his hair and frowned, reminding me of Henry. I felt much closer to this new, worried young man, and quite able to cope with the emergency.

'It will mean complete isolation here, with the children, till we reach Bombay. Only their mothers will be allowed to visit them. You don't have to agree, for it's not in your contract. You may find yourself stuck in hospital in Bombay if you develop measles during the voyage,' he warned me.

'I'll take a chance.' It was my usual answer and came automatically now. The children had stopped their play, and stood around, wide-eyed and solemn.

'Deidre Browning is already isolated with her mother, but it's too late, of course, the mischief is done. Well, it's a short incubation period, so we can expect at least a dozen to come out in spots within the next few days. We shall have to turn this nursery into an isolation ward, with mattresses on the floor, and you in charge. I'll speak to Lowry about it and get it arranged. Afraid you must keep away from the dining saloon. Your meals can be sent down to you in the cabin. The mothers and nannies must have a rota to relieve you.'

He was certainly anticipating a bad epidemic, I thought, but he was probably right, for all the children under ten had played together all day. Only the infants had been spared any contact. But it was surprisingly useful to my shrinking morale, to have this additional responsibility, and I thrived, rather than wilted, at the thought of nursing a roomful of spotted children!

The children went down like ninepins, and seemed to share my enjoyment in the novelty of turning the nursery into an isolation ward. The majority had a mild attack of measles, with a few spots, running noses and sore eyes. But the two lively little Bachelors and the eldest of the Grant children were quite seriously affected. Smothered in a bright pink rash, they ran high temperatures, and could not bear the light for several days. Their anxious mothers shared the vigil during the day, and two of the nannies, whose charges had now joined the rest, took over for several hours during the night.

The voyage that had started so disastrously for me had entirely changed, by this unexpected emergency. We sailed across a calm sea and the sun shone brilliantly. The handful of children who escaped measles—including the frail-looking mite who had also escaped sea-sickness—played happily on the aft deck, with swings and toys, supervised by the mothers. Squatting on a mat, outside the nursery door, Boy awaited instructions to fetch fresh supplies of lemon barley, oranges and ice cream.

We were soon organised like a regiment, and nobody grumbled or complained. In my isolation I was happy and useful. If I had 'blotted my copy book' at the start, all was forgiven. I was a rotten sailor, they said of me, but quite a good nurse! Even the Purser had mellowed and actually thanked me for 'volunteering'.

The hours in dock at Port Said were hot, tedious, and nerve-wracking for all of us confined to the ship. Coal dust covered every inch of the decks, and filtered through every crack. Port holes were closed, and electric fans stirred the hot air round the children's flushed faces. They were bad-tempered and miserable all that day, and I longed for the return to normal conditions.

For six interminable hours, we listened to the chanting of scores of natives, as they climbed the planks with baskets of coal on their heads. They were so thin I could count their ribs, and their pink eyelids glistened under a heavy coating of coal dust. My heart ached for them. They seemed to have no status at all, and even our own Lascars spat on them. Trotting on their bare black feet, they sang their sad monotonous chant, like the slaves of Babylon.

The Third Mate, directing a fresh supply of citrus fruits into the hold, waved and smiled agreeably from the boat deck. He was still a strange, remote figure, and I had to admire him from a distance. A smile, a wave, a frown, nothing more. His charm, for me, was not in his dark distinction, or strange aloofness, but in the extraordinary gentleness of his voice, for it contrasted so strongly with his appearance. He walked with a prowling arrogance, and had clearly enjoyed the howling gale. But he obviously regarded me as nothing more than a novice.

For the rest of the voyage I slept on deck, and nobody raised the slightest objection. Tucked in a couple of deck chairs, I slept fitfully, with many interruptions. Young engineers and quarter-masters, coming off duty, stayed to chat about their homes, mothers and sweethearts. I watched and waited for a glimpse of my hero, but he seemed to be avoiding any further encounter and left me to the boys.

*   *   *   *   *

Taking my daily exercise on the strip of starboard deck, I glanced at the banks of the Suez Canal, with nothing more than a mild curiosity. My mind seemed quite detached from the voyage, for I was now so completely involved with the sick children that I had to remind myself that it was intended to be the thrill of a lifetime.

The barren desert waste had been unchanged in a thousand years. Port Said was the Gateway to the East, 'Chips' had informed me. At the age of sixty, he had no fear of measles, and often came to peep in the open windows of the nursery, to make the children laugh with his clowning.

The Gateway to the East?

I could see now what he meant. We had left behind the Western world and its young civilisation, to steal quietly back into this ageless period of time, long before the birth of Christ. Slipping back into this old civilisation, I was quite calm and unmoved by any strong emotion, for the sense of having seen it all before soothed and refreshed, but did not excite me. Buffeted by the gales, and terrified by the mountainous seas of our Western world, I was glad and relieved to know I was going due East, and need not give it a thought for another three months.

This was where Father had been. His spirit walked beside me now, on my solitary evening exercise. I knew he had not died, I knew I should find him again, somewhere East of Suez. He had been expecting me for years, but time stood still in this sandy waste, and it was but yesterday that he passed this way. I recognised him immediately—the same curling, red hair, the twinkling blue eyes, the waxed moustaches, and the strutting walk. I heard his rip-roaring masculine laugh, and felt the warmth in his strong arms as he gathered me up. 'Darling—darling—darling'—that lovely word he used. Nobody had called me 'darling' since I was twelve. Tender, quick-tempered, kind and cruel. He was all this, but, for me, so *alive*. If he had suggested to me now that we take one of those camels on the bank, and ride away, over the shifting sands, I would not have hesitated for a single moment. He was happy now that this restless spirit could wander unrebuked, unchecked to the end of time. He knew every thought in my head, and felt every quickening pulse, for I was his daughter, flesh of his flesh, and bone of his bone.

Feeling Father so close, I knew that the pattern of all my rash impulses was inherited from him, and that my love for a stranger was not so surprising. Reason had no part in it, only intuition. It was time, I supposed, that I began to experiment with my own dormant sexual sense—dormant by my very ignorance and fear. But now, at last, suddenly awakened to the physical attractions of the Third Mate, I was no longer shy or afraid.

A glimpse of his dark shapely head, at the officers' table in the dining saloon, would set my heart racing. I shadowed him everywhere—an eager, inquisitive shadow, waiting to be noticed! He seemed elusive. Was he bored or flattered?

Scraps of information, artfully gleaned from 'Sparks', Chef, 'Chips' and the young Quarter-Master, fed my infatuation, on this first eventful voyage to India. He was country born and bred—just like me! He was a lone wolf, fearless in storm and in port—gentle in manner and speech, a cricket and rugger enthusiast, a strong swimmer, and a 'man's man'—not a flirt!

Possessed of all these virtues, and so incredibly handsome, why should he notice me? I was too naive, too insignificant, too ordinary. To complement his tall dark distinction he would need a beautiful blonde, I told myself. But I followed his day to day activities so closely I knew exactly where he was to be found every hour of the day! I had only to lift my eyes to the bridge, at 'eight bells', to see him standing there, searching the sea and the sky, or talking with the young Quarter-Master. How I envied him! How I wished the shipping company enrolled Quarter-Mistresses, then I would volunteer!

'The Third Mate is a man's man, the Second is a lady's man, and the First, a bit of a dark horse!' said 'Sparks', conversationally, one evening after dinner. He walked with me from the dining saloon to the companion-way leading to his own little domain on the boat deck. It was not seemly for one of officer rank to associate with the lower orders, but 'Sparks', the gentle father figure who smoothed my rough passage with kindly advice and a twinkle in his eye, was not disposed to avoid me, or anyone else for that matter.

'A man's man,' I repeated, when he had climbed out of sight and left me alone on the aft deck, to dream. I was off-duty, but not allowed to change my clothes, or partake of any entertainment. As a member of the lower orders I had no more status or distinction than I had at the Vicarage as 'between maid' at the age of fourteen! Enviously, I would watch the couples dancing—the pretty girls and elegant women in evening dress, often partnered by 'Young Sparks', the doctor, the purser, and the three officers not on duty on the bridge. When I caught a glimpse of the Third Mate, wearing a bow tie and immaculate white uniform, my throat tightened with pain and I crept away, for I could not bear to watch him holding another woman in his arms.

'It's all part of the job, my dear. Officers are expected to help entertain the passengers in the evening, and, of course, they flirt a bit. It's natural, with all that flattery around. It does nobody any harm, and it's all over in a matter of twenty-five days!' said 'Sparks', puffing on his pipe with quiet unconcern. But the Third Mate was a 'man's man', I reminded myself—determined to keep his image unblemished by such frivolity! That could explain his reluctance to make my acquaintance, and his solitary walks on the boat deck. I excused him everything. He was truly 'Master of his fate, Captain of his soul'.

* * * * *

'I want a drink'—'I want to be excused'—'I want to be sick!' So demanding, all of them, and so self-important since they developed measles.

The Lascars were draping tarpaulin over the aft deck.

'It's bloody hot in the Red Sea!' said 'Chips', who appeared to be directing operations.

The Lascars folded my deck chairs and play-pens, and picked up all the rubbish the children had left behind. They smiled shyly and sweetly. In my own little world I was spoiled and flattered: Chef reserved tasty morsels of turkey and trifle for my tray; Joe Bates had brought a box of Turkish Delight from a merchant in Port Said (so horrible I dropped it surreptitiously overboard); even the Purser had taken to smiling at me.

So we sailed across the Indian Ocean, and I had to remind myself whenever I walked that narrow strip of deck that it really was the Indian Ocean.

The few fortunate children who had escaped measles spent most of the day hopping in and out of the small swimming pool on the foredeck, with fond mothers and nannies in attendance. Adult passengers lounged in deck chairs, and the hearty individuals changed their 'ten times round the deck before dinner' to six times round the deck before breakfast.

'Next stop—Bombay!' yelled Joe Bates, and added fervently, 'Thank Gawd!'

'Young Sparks', a bit of a dandy in his tropical uniform, revelled in the sun, and had conquered several hearts. He was getting more and more conceited. Always immaculate, with his cap at a jaunty angle, he strolled nonchalantly about the boat deck.

'You wait till we get him ashore. We'll take the mickey out of him!' promised a young Quarter-Master, with a reputation for devilment.

The last five days and nights of the voyage were saturated by sunshine and moonlight. We glided along with nothing more than a gentle purr from the engines. Flying fishes darted like dragon-flies in gauzy scintillating colours, and porpoises played happily in school, to the huge delight of the children. But that was all. We apparently shared the Indian Ocean with the porpoises and the flying fishes. The horizon was limitless. We could go on and on for ever, I thought, with momentary panic early one morning, for I had a strange dread of the words 'for ever'.

Would my relationship with the Third Mate never develop? Fresh tactics must be employed. He *must* notice me! To be accepted by the rest, and ignored by the Third Mate, was a fresh challenge to my insatiable appetite!

Everything I said to the others was directed at him personally now, for everyone gossiped among themselves, like women over a hedge, or on their doorsteps. In this small world, so far removed from home, family and friends, their talk concerned small matters, rather than profound philosophy.

Reverting back to the old recklessness and rebellion against authority, I knew my behaviour would be discussed with interest and amusement. But now I was a child again, child-like in behaviour—'showing off' with the old desire to get attention.

'Sparks' had a word with me. 'What's this I hear about a young woman being seen in the swimming pool with a crowd of men, at two o'clock in the morning? It couldn't be you, of course, for the pool is out-of-bounds to the staff and crew, isn't that so, my dear?'

'I believe it is,' I answered innocently, but a fit of giggles gave me away. 'They dared me, Sparks, and I can't resist a dare, but it was no picnic, I can tell you. I had to crawl on my hands and knees under all the windows on the port side, and wait for a cloud to cover the moon! I was shivering when they finally dragged me into the water. It's chilly at two o'clock in the morning, even in the Indian Ocean!'

'You've got a bloody nerve!' said Sparks, feelingly.

'That's the second time you've reminded me.'

'Well, for God's sake take care, you were seen from the bridge.'

'Who saw me?'

'The Third Mate.'

I smiled complacently.

'*He* wouldn't report me,' I told Sparks.

But in my quiet moments, alone on the top bunk in the stuffy cabin, I was miserably aware of my mistake.

Attraction should be a subtle sense, touched with magic and mystery—not a noisy, boisterous bid for attention!

Perhaps in the mystic realms of the East, the forces of Destiny would bring us together? Romance would blossom when uniforms were discarded, and our true selves revealed. I smiled and hugged the pillow—damp with tears and sweat, never dry!

Darling—darling—darling.

Such a lovely word, I could hardly wait to use it!

* * * * *

The sun beat down mercilessly on the ship as she lay alongside the wide quay in Bombay Harbour. Sweating passengers waited impatiently for the Health Authorities to give permission to go ashore. Army personnel, angry and agitated business executives and missionaries, bored with the passage and ready for action, clamoured at the Purser's office. Electric fans blew draughty blasts of hot air; stewards and stewardesses served iced drinks and iced coffee. But the tension grew and the atmosphere was charged with rebellion.

These familiar people we had seen all around us for twenty-five days were suddenly strangers. They looked at us with hostile eyes, as though our innocent uniforms put us in the same category as the officers of the Health Authorities and Customs and Excise. We were rejected and despised 'servants of the public'—incompetent, inconsiderate, with enough red tape to hang ourselves! The blonde's irate husband threatened to report us all to the 'Governor'—a distant relative of his wife's family of whom much mention had been made during the voyage. It was disgusting and disgraceful, he argued, to be compelled to hang around all day in such sweltering heat: we thought so too!

When, at last, the children who were still infectious had been taken by ambulance to hospital, and the passengers disembarked, we hardly had the strength to raise a hand in salute. Our smiles faded, huge sighs of relief tore from our parched lips, as the last impatient figure hurried down the gangway. Cars and taxis slid away in a cloud of white dust.

Then we snatched off our caps and uniform and flung ourselves down to rest on our bunks, under the whirring fans. The heat was intense. The final day of the voyage had been even more exacting to our nerves and patience than the first. Then all was quiet. The ship was no longer a live creature with a pulsing heart, but a dead shell, lying motionless under the burning sun.

In cotton pants and petticoat, I sprawled uncomfortably on the top bunk. Exhausted in mind and body, I seemed to be drained dry of every emotion. The long voyage and the long vigil was over. It had been interminable. Now the load of responsibility and the exacting demands of the children had been removed, I was near to tears. Where was the thrill and excitement of my first glimpse of Bombay? What had happened to me en route that I felt nothing but tears in my eyes and a lump in my throat? On my bunk, of all places, and empty of feeling, with this magical city of the East on our doorstep! Could there be a more disappointing anticlimax to the years of sweet anticipation?

Annie Bunce, draped in a loose Japanese kimono, allowed her ponderous breasts to sag comfortably.

'Well, that's got rid of that lot!' she told me, with some satisfaction. Five minutes later she was snoring!

* * * * *

I woke refreshed and eager to sample the new day, and hurried on deck to inspect our surroundings. In place of the dreary, wet-flagged quay of our embarkation port, I saw a sun-drenched quay, with a back-cloth of shimmering white mosques and minarets. A peculiar, elusive smell—the smell of India?—mingled with the smell of an English breakfast of bacon and eggs and toast. Slight, dark-skinned figures glided about the wharf and wandered around the sheds. Unhurried, noiseless, barefoot, they contrasted strangely with the porters and dockers of Liverpool. A white dust sprinkled everything as thoroughly as the black coal dust had sprinkled every inch of dock and deck at Port Said.

And now, at last, I had time to stand and stare—to recognise this land so long familiar in my imagination. I was no stranger to India, with Father's vivid pictures drawn on my memory. I have been here before, I thought, as I leaned on the rail, feasting my eyes on the scene below. Later on in the day it would be unbearably hot, and everyone, including the native porters, would sleep in the shade. But now, in the early morning, I felt the warmth wrapping me round in a healing, beneficial cloak.

It was something of a shock at the breakfast table to be reminded that I had to spend four hours that morning sorting dirty linen for the laundry at Bombay, and four hours on subsequent mornings in dock repairing linen, with two senior stewardesses, This, to me, was a flagrant violation of my contract. I had already discharged my duties as a children's stewardess, and looked forward to the fun that had been promised me.

My shipmates were tickled to death, when I drifted into breakfast attired in a dainty muslin dress, with smart sandals and bare legs. Gusts of laughter greeted me. The senior

77

stewardesses, respectfully dressed in white overalls and stockings, looked askance at my bare legs.

'Where do you think you are going?' Mrs Hammond asked, smothering a giggle.

'Ashore!'

Annie Bunce choked on a grilled tomato and 'Chips' chuckled happily.

'You are a caution, and no mistake! Didn't nobody ever tell you then, that we all 'as to work part day in port?'

Speechless with indignation, I allowed Boy to fetch my breakfast. He was also grinning, I noticed. Looking round on their frank, familiar faces, I suddenly realised they had seen it all before so many times it was no longer a novelty to be sitting in the saloon of a ship docked in Bombay harbour. Only the young engineer and myself were novices. To the rest it was just a job of work. The novelty had worn off years ago. There was nothing left to surprise, excite or interest them. For me, everything was new, but nobody shared my enthusiasm. They sat there, completely unmoved by any emotion, other than amusement, stolidly eating an English breakfast. The men argued about Arsenal and Spurs, and the two stewardesses decided to go to the pictures that evening.

'There's a seaman's club here. We can get a good game of snooker and a decent glass of beer,' said the young Quarter-Master.

My heart sank. We may as well be back in Liverpool! Work all morning, sleep all afternoon, then a choice of evening entertainment—a film with the two stewardesses or the seaman's club with the boys!

I decided to explore the city that same afternoon as soon as my superiors were safely asleep.

*   *   *   *   *

'Mad dogs and Englishmen—and presumably English girls —go out in the midday sun!' A cool, appraising voice accosted me at the dockyard gates. A good-looking customs officer, in immaculate tropical uniform, opened the car door.

'Hop in! We'll go and buy you a topee, my girl, before we have you fainting with the heat!' he said authoritatively—so in I hopped.

The sentries saluted smartly as we swept through the gates.

'You have *got* a pass, I suppose? You'll need it you know to get in and out of these gates. Can't have every Tom, Dick and Harry wandering around His Majesty's Docks!'

'No, I haven't a pass. As a matter of fact, I sneaked out,' I confessed.

'Then your luck's in, my child, for you wouldn't get past those chaps on the gate without one.'

'Are you bringing me back, then?'

'Of course. Should I abandon an attractive young woman in a strange city? Beside's, it's not done. You mustn't think of wandering around on your own. You must take a taxi if I'm not around. You'll see what I mean in a moment.'

I saw and gasped. The streets around the docks were slums of a kind I had never seen or imagined. Seething with humanity, a horrible stench rose in waves of nauseating suffocation from the dust. Bundles of filthy rags sprawled on the pavements, and protruding from the rags were scraggy arms and legs, without flesh. Splashes of scarlet surrounded them.

'They're bleeding!' I whispered. 'Look at the blood.'

'Betel nut. They chew it and spit it out,' my companion explained complacently.

I shuddered and felt quite sick with revulsion.

'It's not all mosques, palaces and pomp. There is most appalling poverty in India. In less than five minutes we shall be out of this and driving into a prosperous city, with wide boulevards, luxury flats, American automobiles and expensive restaurants. It's a country of contrasts, poverty and riches. The beggar will be begging for alms exactly as he was doing two thousand years ago. Appalling poverty and immense wealth—that's India,' my companion told me.

The India of my imagination, built on Father's vivid descriptions, photographs and diaries, was a romantic country. Blind beggars and pitiful bundles of starved humanity had no place in it. I had seen the magic and mystery, but not the misery. It had been painted for me in vivid colours, rich and luxurious, but never in these sombre shades, where Englishmen drove past quickly, holding disdainful noses against the stench.

This man beside me had the same arrogance as Father. He spoke with the same authority. He was a white Sahib. Obviously the white Sahib was a person of some importance, a superior being, for I had seen his superiority displayed on board ship, in no uncertain manner. Joe Bates was a bully who shouted and swore at those under him. Two of the officers addressed the Lascars with less regard than they had for their dogs or cats. Only the Chef was kind, and his boys adored him, and served him with love and not fear. All this I had seen with my own eyes on the outward voyage, and been surprised and disgusted.

'Forget it! Let's have a drink, or an ice cream soda, at this bar on the corner. By the way, what's your name?'

I was still dazed and shocked by these first impressions, and answered him absently.

'Sarah Shears.'

'My name's Blake—Richard Blake.'

We shook hands formally, after that rather belated introduction. Then he took my arm, and guided me to a table in the shaded bar. It was cool and comfortable, and my first ice cream soda deliciously cold. Richard Blake drank whisky and soda. Without the topee he looked no more than twenty-five. His fair skin was tanned a golden brown, and his blond hair was sleek and shining.

'I'm glad I ran into you,' he was saying. 'I'll show you around. It will be fun! I don't often get the opportunity of meeting someone fresh from home. Did you see me yesterday? I saw you, and Lowry told me you were new to the job, and this was, in fact, your first voyage. He said you had shaped pretty well, considering most of the kids went down with measles. Well drink up, and I'll order another. Then to the bazaar to get that topee!'

'Don't you ever do any work, Richard Blake!' I teased.

'Of course I work, all kinds of odd hours. Got to see a Swedish cargo ship in tonight. She docks about ten, alongside yours, as a matter of fact. But I shall be free all day to-morrow. We could take a run out to the coast and bathe.'

He was so accustomed to giving orders it didn't occur to him I might have other plans.

'I'm working till noon,' I reminded him.

'Blast!'

'But I could see you later. We only have ten days here, and there is so much I want to see. Apart from the Seventh Engineer, I'm the only novice. All the rest have seen it all before so many times, they could be in Blackpool for all the notice they take!'

'You poor kid!'

He drained his glass, threw a coin on the table, and followed me out. His swaggering importance was part of his charm, and his lordly manner in the native bazaar bought instant attention.

'Mem-sahib wishes to buy a topee, but none of your fancy prices, my good man,' he began, adding to me,' They are all a bunch of crooks. Beat them down and never give them what they ask.'

I quaked under such a bold attack and wished he had left me to my own devices. A little crowd of interested spectators stopped to enjoy the diversion, and I was soon the centre of attraction, as a dozen or more topees were tried on my head. Dark-eyed women, draped in saris, smiled encouragement, as the shop-keeper patiently sought for the right fitting. His hands were as gentle as his voice, and he tried first one, then another on my obstinate brown head. Still Richard Blake was not entirely satisfied, and the little man disappeared behind the beaded screen for the third time, obedient to the young Sahib's instructions. At last I had had enough, for one topee seemed the same as any other. They were all ugly, unbecoming, and made me feel quite ridiculous.

'I'll have this one, thank you,' I said firmly.

Then the bargaining commenced. Richard Blake argued and the shop keeper pleaded. I wandered away to look at some brasses, and left them to settle it between them, for I had decided it was both rude and embarrassing. My companion emerged at length, flushed with success.

'You see what I mean? I got it for two-thirds of the original price, the old scoundrel!'

I pressed money into his hand, but he thrust it back.

'My pleasure, Sarah,' he said.

I was fascinated by the native bazaar, and he could not get me away. My eyes were ravished by yards of Indian silk, in brilliant colours and designs, richly embroidered curtains, mosaic ornaments, vases, jewellery and exquisite fans. Amongst the brasses I recognised several replicas of the souvenirs which Father had brought home.

'You wish to buy, Mem-sahib? I show you plenty more,

beautiful new consignment!' the wheedling voice asked plaintively.

My purse was bursting with the annas and rupees the Purser had exchanged for my English notes. All the mothers had given me presents and I felt enormously rich and prosperous. I had to buy *something*, if only to prove I had actually *been* to the native bazaar!

'I'll have that little green tin for my biscuits, and an ash tray, though I don't smoke, and a baby elephant for a lucky mascot, and some beads, though I never wear them,' I decided.

Richard Blake protested strongly, then walked away in a huff, for I paid the full price for my purchases to the huge delight of the toothless little man in a grubby turban, who called all the blessings of Allah on my head, and bowed me ceremoniously on to the pavement. My companion was loitering rather sulkily on the kerb, and obviously bored with the bazaar and my naive enjoyment.

'I'm sorry, but I hate all that bargaining. It's so undignified.'

He took my arm and propelled me firmly towards the car.

We drove in silence for a few minutes, and I waited for him to speak. Then he smiled at me, and turning his head said,

'I should have known better. A girl who would take as many risks as you seem to have taken in the past few months, would naturally have a mind of her own! Am I forgiven for being so boorish?'

'Of course. You were only trying to help. Where are we going?'

'Malabar Hill—to breathe some fresh air. I think we both need it. Besides, it's a truly magnificent view from the top and you can see the city spread out at your feet.'

'I must be back on board for staff supper at six.'

'I'll get you back, don't worry.'

Some time later, we sat on a low wall, looking down on the city. His arm lay lightly across my shoulders, and my face burned under the topee.

'I want to kiss you—do you mind?'

I knew I should not care for his kisses any more than I cared for his sulks or superiority.

'Shall we go back?' I asked, innocently.

A dozen faces looked up expectantly from the staff table in the saloon.

'Well, my girl, and what have you been up to *this* time?' Chef demanded, affably.

At the officers' table I could see 'Young Sparks' talking animatedly with the Third Mate, and the Chief Engineer, in a tropical suit, looking absurdly like Spencer Tracy. The young doctor, relieved at last of his responsibilities, was laughing at one of the Second Mate's rather dubious jokes.

I sat down at our table, to tell the story of my adventurous afternoon, but my eyes strayed repeatedly to that dark hand-head at the other table.

'You *are* coming to the Seamen's Club with us tonight, I take it?' the young Quarter-Master was asking, 'or have you made made another engagement with the new heart-throb?'

'Och, you must come, Sarah,' the 'Seventh' added decisively.

We both had the same unsophisticated background; the same innocence, the same immaturity. We had shared a pot of tea, in the sheltered corner of the deck, during the early days of my solitary isolation, when the infected children slept in rows on the nursery floor. We had swopped stories about our village, our families, our way of life.

'What are we doing here, Jock?' I asked him once, 'we must be crazy?'

His rare smile flickered across his freckled face. He had fallen down a companion-way and broken two teeth, during the gale.

'Och, but we've got to see the worrrld!' he told me, with a glint in his eyes. 'We canna sit down on our backsides till we've had a wee excursion!'

One way and another, I had grown quite fond of Jock, so when his voice reached me from the end of the table—'Och, you must come, Sarah,'—I dragged my thoughts and my eyes from that dark distinguished head, at the officers' table, and answered,

'I should love to come.'

Mrs Hammond informed me, with the cool condescension of one who has escaped such coarse frivolities, that I should find the Seamen's Club crowded and rowdy, with a mix-ture of nationalities, and a few rough characters inclined to drunkenness. But the boys were upset, and shouted indignantly that their club was nothing of the kind. All the clientele would be sober, well-mannered and orderly, they assured me.

Well, I didn't really mind *how* they behaved as long as I had Jock, Mac, Bill, Pat and funny old 'Chips' to protect me!

'Meet you in half-an-hour, and we won't take a taxi— we'll take a gharrie and have fun!' promised Bill, the Second Steward, who had done it all before, but was not yet blasé.

I followed Jock down the gangway, at an hour when I usually climbed into my bunk. There were no restrictions at all apparently. We were free now to do exactly as we pleased, providing we reported for our four-hour duty period at 8 a.m.

The boys were waiting on the quay, with a gharrie, and urged me to hurry, before the driver fell asleep again! They pushed me into the dusty little cab, and fell in after me, with whoops of joy and excitement. Pat, the cheeky Quarter-Master, climbed on the driver's seat, and shouted authoritatively,

'Seamen's Club—and make it snappy!'

The face beside him was wrinkled like a prune, and it lifted slowly from the thin chest.

'Come on, Methuselah, get moving!' urged Pat impatiently, giving the old man a shake that nearly toppled him off the seat. Accustomed to this rough treatment from the young Sahibs, he merely smiled ingratiatingly—a wide toothless smile, made some mild protest about the crowded vehicle, and flicked the mule's flanks with a whip. We had all remembered to bring our passes and flourished them haughtily under the noses of the two sentries at the gate.

'Chips' had offered me a seat on his bony knees, and we rocked and jolted over the cobblestones. Suddenly we were conscious of this wonderful feeling of escape from officialdom and our senior officers who were always ready to pounce on some offender. Jock was as gay as his serious nature would allow, and ready for anything his more experienced shipmates might suggest—within reason, of course!

'I am not intending to associate with lassies of dubious reputation,' he had confided to me, with great earnestness.

It was rather crowded and rowdy at the Seamen's Club, and I didn't much enjoy being snatched from one partner to another, in a sort of perpetual 'Paul Jones'. A few dusky-skinned, black-eyed girls shared the dubious honour of being much sought after as dancing partners, for the men out-numbered the girls by twenty to one. Blond Swedes, slant-eyed Chinese, solemn Dutch, and hilarious French seamen hugged me round the waist, trampled on my new sandals, and whirled me round the dance hall in a temperature more suited to lazy relaxation in a hammock! The boys drank enormous quantities of iced beer, and provided me with endless ice cream sodas.

The hours dragged by. Only Bill remained on the edge of the dance floor, passionately hugging a lovely little half-caste, from whom he flatly refused to be separated. I saw him pushing away several intended rivals, rather truculently. The rest had disappeared, either to the bar, or to play snooker. I suppose they had decided that since I had so many partners I must be enjoying myself. It seemed a pity to disillusion them, or to suggest going back to the ship on their first night ashore, but I began to feel a little desperate.

Searching the sea of strange faces around me, my eyes were drawn towards an open french window. In the midst of a crowd of interested spectators, a tall distinguished figure stood out prominently. I felt myself trembling in the clumsy grasp of a huge giant of a man in an open-neck shirt. His hairy chest, exposed and scorched by the sun, filled me with loathing. If this was 'having fun' I had had enough! My head throbbed and my stomach rebelled at the over in-dulgence of ice cream sodas.

'Excuse me,' said the cool, bland voice—and I was dragged from under the hairy chest, to the wide-flung windows.

Outside, in the cool night air, my companion regarded my crumpled appearance with undisguised amusement.

'I thought you were definitely wilting and it was high time somebody rescued you!' he chuckled. He was still clutching my hot, sticky hand.

My sandals were ruined, my hair dishevelled, and beads of perspiration dripped off my nose. Why does he always have to see me when I'm looking a mess, I thought miserably.

Without any explanation he handed me a clean, folded handkerchief, and I carefully wiped my face and hands.

'The boys are happily playing snooker, and Bill seems to be

enjoying himself. I'll tell them I will deliver you safely back to the ship,' he told me, with infuriating superiority.

'But I don't want to go back yet!' I protested. 'Surely this isn't the only attraction in Bombay?'

He considered the matter, thoughtfully.

'We could have a look at Malabar Hill. It's one of the recognised sights, and the air is certainly pure.'

I did not mention I had already sampled the air of Malabar Hill, but pretended a great interest in the place. *Anywhere* would be paradise, I thought, with him alone.

Now, at last, we were together. There might not be another opportunity before we were back on duty, en route to Karachi. Only ten nights in Bombay.

'Come along then, and we'll find a gharrie'.

I had almost to run to catch up with his long, prowling stride.

I would not mention a word about the Customs Officer, I decided, or he might suppose I was a shocking flirt. It didn't occur to me, till later, that *everything* was news on board ship, especially in dock, so of course he was already aware of my escapade.

I sat beside him in the jolting gharrie, looking down at our clasped hands; all my emotions were entwined in adoration of this gentle, quiet stranger, and could not be expressed. The silence was broken by the sound of the mule's hooves on the cobbles, and the swish of the whip on its thin flanks. To speak would have broken the spell of this enchanted ride, on a warm tropical night, under a sky studded with a million stars.

I sighed rapturously, and his cool hand squeezed mine in response.

But he was not in love with me.

He did not even want to kiss me.

He was just being kind. I had to remind myself of this, repeatedly, for it was the truth—the bitter, cruel truth.

* * * * *

We dined and danced together the following night, at the smartest hotel in Bombay. But he was still not in love with me. He was just being kind. It must have been embarrassing to be so idolised.

It was almost a relief to get back into uniform, and a schedule of duties again.

'Next stop—Karachi!' yelled Joe Bates.

In Karachi I had friends—a family of Anglo-Indians I had met on board. They came to collect me every afternoon on the quay in a sleek grey car, to enjoy the warm hospitality of their family life.

By inter-marriage, they had no status at all. Neither the British, nor the high-caste Indians accepted them, and they lived apart, in rather sad isolation, I noticed, but found their happiness in the family. Their house was cool and comfortable, with rush mats on the floors, and quiet servants drifting about with easy, unhurried grace.

'The one who sweeps the floor does not wash the dishes, the servant who washes the dishes does not wash the clothes, and so on and so forth,' my hostess explained carelessly.

Their picnics were planned and organised to the last detail. After the siesta, family and friends piled into cars, while the servants filled the boots with enough food to feed a regiment. Iced drinks, ice-creams and iced coffee were included, and even a spirit stove for brewing tea!

We drove in a convoy beyond the airport, to a cool plantation on the edge of the Sind desert. Green bananas hung in bunches on the bushes over a wide area, watered by artificial canals. We camped under an enormous banyan tree, with spreading branches.

The youngest member of the party, aged seven, was a fair-skinned, blue-eyed boy destined for boarding school in England the following year. This child, with the charming manners and intelligence he had inherited from his father's people, was soon to be reminded that he was not a thoroughbred. I could foresee an English girl falling in love with this child grown to man-hood. Would she in turn bear a fair or a dark-skinned child, or a child neither dark nor fair, with a parchment skin and pale amber-flecked eyes—an Anglo-Indian?

Human relationships were so frail, and love so strangely inexplicable.

I faced the future reluctantly now, because I knew it might not hold the one man I wanted—still a stranger after six interminable weeks. Was the attraction only physical then? If so, had I been deceived into thinking it was spiritual, by my very innocence? I had much to learn about the mystery of sex. It had not been explained, and I had been too scared to experiment.

It was such a lovely picnic and everyone made a great fuss of me, but now I could think of nothing else but getting back to the ship.

I *had* to see him, alone—*tonight*!

*   *   *   *   *

He was stretched on his bunk, in silk pyjamas, reading a book. His eyes blazed, and he sat up, leaning on one elbow. He was no longer gentle, and not even kind.

'Tell me,' he said, with menacing directness, 'are you still a virgin?'

I nodded, mutely.

'Then get the hell out of here!' he told me—and I fled.

*   *   *   *   *

On the homeward voyage most of our passengers were embarking at Karachi, and sailing day dawned for me again, in reverse.

After the Liverpool initiation, I knew what to expect, and felt much more confident. It was necessary to put on the same bold front as the rest of my shipmates. We were all acting a part, I realised now.

The official masks had been removed, together with the smart uniforms, in port. Everyone's ordinary selves had emerged unfettered by restrictions and the stern discipline of life aboard ship. I had joined them on midnight bathes in the warm sea, when the status distinction that divided them on duty was disregarded in a pair of trunks. Who could tell a junior officer from a subordinate, when they played around like a school of porpoises?

Senior officers, however, still conducted themselves with great decorum, even in port. I had scarcely seen them for the past three weeks. Where did they go? What did they do in Bombay and Karachi?

Shore leave was a welcome diversion for a few weeks, but I think they enjoyed getting back into their uniforms again, retrieving their lost dignity and superiority. I remembered them at Liverpool, one by one, stepping briskly out of taxis, on the quayside, and marching purposefully up the gangway. There was no reluctance in their hurrying steps, only eagerness.

I had been refused permission to stay in India and transfer my services from a shipping company to a private family. Several of the mothers, whose children I had nursed through measles, had offered me a temporary post as nannie. I had a choice of Calcutta, Bangalore, or the North West Frontier, and chose the latter for its colourful association with romantic heroes of film and fiction! This, to me, was the golden opportunity to extend my travels, for I had no hope of ever acquiring enough money to travel independently.

Yet by 'working my passage' I was tied to a contract it was impossible to break, as the Purser informed me with raised eyebrows.

'Stay in India? Whatever next?'

Clearly he considered my request not only extremely bad taste, but utterly crazy. 'Sparks' was more sympathetic. He reappeared on the boat-deck with his pipe and cheery greeting the day prior to sailing. I had seen him only briefly during this period, taking leisurely meals with the other senior officers, or going ashore with the Chief Engineer. He listened to my tale of frustrated hopes, with tolerant amusement.

'North Western Frontier, eh? Sounds exciting, but a bit of a trouble spot, actually. Never quite sure who is coming over the border from Afghanistan. Hordes of tribesmen—fierce devils, might get your throat cut.' He puffed a cloud of fragrant smoke, and patted my hand. 'You come back with us, my dear, it's safer. Besides, I like having you around,' he added kindly.

I sighed. 'You don't understand, Sparkie. There's another reason, a private reason, why I should like to stay out here for a year or two.'

'Yes, my dear, I know.'

My face burned and my breath caught in my throat.

'He hasn't? He didn't?'

'No, he hasn't said a word to anyone.'

I breathed again.

'Was it so obvious?'

He nodded, and tears flooded my eyes.

'He's not free, Sarah—even if he loved you. He's engaged to marry a girl in Cape Town.'

'Even . . . if . . he loved . . . me . .' I wailed forlornly. 'Sparkie dear, why do I always fall in love with someone who sees me only as a child, not a woman? This is the second time! it's so humiliating!'

He gave me a shoulder to cry on, and some very sound advice.

'Next time, my dear, leave the hunting to the male. It's instinctive.'

*   *   *   *   *

The passage home was almost uneventful, till we ran into something called the Gulf Stream outside the harbour at Marseilles. Then I was attacked with the old nausea, and so was Jock, poor lad!

But we had seen Stromboli and the Straits of Messina bathed in sunshine, while little white villas climbed the hills on either shore. We had seen a shark, or was it a sword-fish? We had tasted exotic fruits and received our mail in every port.

'What's that, for heaven's sake?' I asked 'Chips' early one morning, pointing to the horizon.

'That's the Rock of Gibraltar.'

'The Bank of England—or course—firm as the Rock of Gibraltar.'

'That's right,' he agreed. 'Ow's the old tum be'aving? Bit squeamish, eh?'

'Just a bit.'

'Thought so,' he grinned. ''Ave a peppermint?'

My charges on the homeward voyage were decidedly more difficult. Spoiled by adoring ayahs and native servants, they were rude, naughty and disobedient. Children's meals were a nightmare of tears and tantrums. Food was scattered on the floor and the tables. Fond mammas coaxed stubborn small mouths to open, and fed their offspring like birds in a glutinous nest.

Toddlers yelled and struggled on their chairs, older children, en route to boarding school and discipline, ran riot, driving us all to distraction. Remembering the code of conduct for a children's stewardess, I pleaded and persuaded, coaxed and cosseted horrid little boys and girls, who badly needed a good spanking! We had to think of fresh ways and means to keep them amused and entertained.

'Keep smiling!' urged the Purser, chasing three naughty boys out of his office.

'Keep smiling!' said Annie Bunce, stepping over a human train in the alleyway.

'Keep smiling?' groaned Joe Bates. 'What jer think I'm doing then—bloody well crying . . . ?'

* * * * *

It was over.

We had signed off at the shipping office, and now we were going our separate ways, with money to spend, and a period of idleness, before the next trip. It was all very casual.

'So long, Sarah. Be good!'

'Cheerio!'

'Goodbye, my girl.'

'Au revoir!' This from the doctor, who was sailing to Cape Town next month.

The one person I was hoping would say goodbye avoided me. No glance, no smile, no frown, *nothing*! Oh *God*! He walked away without a backward glance.

I called a taxi, and climbed in—dazed and shattered. My body ached so intolerably I thought I must have been beaten (though I had never been beaten in my life). I could almost feel the bruises, I was so sore.

Then it *was* only a physical attraction—a physical ache? Was it because he had rejected me that I suffered this pain?

It was no time for a diagnosis, the wound was too raw.

'Darling—darling—darling.'

Such a lovely word, but wasted. He had not wanted to hear it.

* * * * *

What do I remember of the next three voyages to India? I remember only a sense of utter desolation, when I signed on at Birkenhead, a few weeks later.

Searching the ship for that tall, distinguished figure, the dark, shapely head, and suntanned face, I searched in vain, for he was not there.

'Where's the Third Mate?' I inquired, with assumed casualness, of Annie Bunce.

'On the South African run.'

'Will he be back next trip?'

'Not if he can help it! He's got his girl in Cape Town.'

'Then—then we shan't see him again?' My voice trembled, I felt choked with tears. And then, with a pretence of indifference I said,

'Oh well, I expect we shall manage to survive!'

4

LONDON

The letter I had been expecting for two years arrived one morning from Liverpool;

> 'We regret to inform you that your services as a children's stewardess will no longer be required. We wish to emphasise that this decision in no way reflects on your character and conduct. Regular reports from your senior officers, and the ship's doctor, seem to suggest, however, that your general physique is not strong enough for this kind of work, and that you have been indisposed on every voyage, for several days. As you will fully realise, this entails extra work and responsibility for senior stewardesses, who are obliged to take over your duties. We trust you will soon find a more congenial post ashore.
> With all good wishes for the future. We remain . . . . .'

I handed this letter to Mother without a word, and I knew she was relieved that this precarious passage of my life was over.

I had been idle now for three months, and had spent practically all the money I had earned on my last voyage. Mother had been paid for my board and lodging, and I had stayed at home for these irregular periods between each voyage. Like Father, I had no sense of saving for the inevitable 'rainy day', and the money had not even dwindled away. It had been spent lavishly on presents and holidays. Had Mother really enjoyed her first real holiday away from the family?

She chose it to please me, and we went away together for two weeks.

It rained every day, and the farm she had chosen from a brochure was in North Devon. It was not only remote, but buried in antiquity! We washed ourselves in lukewarm water, in a china basin, wreathed in rose buds. The bathroom geyser was a frightening monster we left alone. We went to bed by candlelight—floorboards creaked and windows rattled. Rain swept the bleak landscape as we breakfasted each morning in the dim parlour, then draped ourselves in mackintoshes to plod through the mud.

'A bus every two hours to Barnstaple, six days a week!' the farmer's wife informed us, with obvious pride in such a regular service.

Undaunted, and saying as often as she could, 'The sun will shine tomorrow,' Mother rallied my dwindling spirits.

Each wretched day, we set forth with a picnic lunch, and fed it to the seagulls, at one or other of the coastal resorts, to which we travelled by bus or coach, from Barnstaple. To sit in a rain-swept shelter on the promenade, or to huddle under a breakwater within sight and sound of the angry grey sea, was too distressing even for Mother.

'Well, it's no sort of weather for picnics, let's find a nice restaurant and have a good, hot meal,' I would suggest.

'Can we afford it?'

'Of course we can afford it!'

'But it's costing much more than you intended?'

'Forget the cost! Let's enjoy ourselves! Shall we go to the pictures this afternoon, or would you prefer the concert party on the pier?'

Considering the choice of two evils, for neither held any appeal for her, Mother would usually choose the concert party. For two lively hours we were entertained in a glittering atmosphere of boisterous hilarity. Mother's face, scarlet with embarrassment at the crude jokes and naughty stories, would pale again, when a nice little scene was enacted from one of the 'refined' classics. Dear Mother!

'Are you enjoying it—the holiday, I mean,' I would ask anxiously, from time to time.

'Very much indeed!'

Her answer never varied, for she would not have me

disappointed after spending so much money. But I was not deceived by her gallant cheerfulness, and I knew we were both counting the days to go back home.

'Only two more days!' I exclaimed impulsively one evening, as we climbed the stairs with our candles, after supper. She did not answer, but her silence was more profound than words.

For years I had dreamed of doing this, and now the weather had ruined it completely. The flames of our two candles flickered on the ceiling, and the wind howled in the empty chimney. I wanted to cry. Mother's comforting arm pressed my shoulder and her lips touched my hair.

'Thank you, Sarah. It was such a kind thought, and I am most grateful.'

I gulped back my tears.

'*Next* time we will go to Scotland, or Ireland, perhaps. Or would you like the Lakes?'

'Scotland would be nice.' She gave me her rare and beautiful smile. But it was our first and our only holiday together.

*　　*　　*　　*　　*

'What will you do now?'

The question everyone was asking.

'I shall live in London,' I heard myself answering, one day, 'and I shall write a novel!' I added defiantly.

'But what will you do—for a living, I mean?' asked Henry, who liked to be assured I was not going to starve in a garret, even supposing I had this queer sort of bee in my bonnet.

I shrugged.

'Anything to pay the rent. I expect to finish my first novel in six months, then I shall make a living with my pen.'

He considered this with grave doubts.

'How can you be so sure?'

'Other writers do.'

'Only if they are *famous*.'

'They all had to start sometime. Anyway, I shall like living in London. It's nearly as good as Paris, for writers and artists—the right sort of atmosphere.'

'You're mad!'

'Yes, I know.'

The day I left for London, Mother presented me with a document.

'You had better take this,' she said resignedly. 'It's an insurance policy I have been paying every week since you were born. I had one for each of you. If you cash it now it will pay your expenses until you are settled in another job.'

I gaped in astonishment.

'Mother! Thank you a thousand times! It's like manna from Heaven!' I exclaimed, excitedly. 'Gosh! I shall have enough to live on for six months, if I budget carefully. Only fifteen shillings a week rent for that bed-sitting room in Bayswater I found in *Dalton's Weekly*. It's near Hyde Park too, so I'll get plenty of fresh air. I shall write all day with walks in the park between the chapters!'

'Well, I suppose you must get it out of your system, if you are ever going to settle down,' she sighed.

'You mean the writing?'

'Yes.'

My heart sank. It was so much a part of me, and so fundamentally necessary to my very existence, I would never be able to 'get it out of my system'.

'But it's my only talent, I must use it, not waste it,' I told her, defensively.

'Well, take care. Look after yourself properly. Have a good dinner every day, and don't forget the vegetables. Drink plenty of milk and make sure the bed is properly aired.'

'Yes, Mother.'

I left her standing there, at the garden gate. She waved till I was out of sight.

What is independence? What is freedom? My heart still clung, at parting, to that strong, indomitable woman. I could not bear to leave her, yet I had to go. She knew at last that I was my Father's daughter, and that it would never be any different.

*　　*　　*　　*　　*

Mrs O'Brien, the housekeeper at Sixty-Two, was out on the front steps bidding a tearful farewell to a young couple laden with bags and bundles. She took no notice of me at all as I climbed out of the taxi, and the driver dumped my suitcases on the pavement.

'They hadn't paid their rent now for three weeks, the poor unlucky creatures, my heart bleeds for them with no place to go but a hostel,' she announced, with a last sniff of sympathy for her poor unfortunate country folk. Then suddenly she was aware of me. 'Glory be!—you must be the new tenant for Number Eight? Come in m'dear. But 'tis more than body and soul can put up with now. All this coming and going, and more like Waterloo Station than a decent, respectable apartment house! I shall be handing in me notice at the end of the month, as sure as me name's Katie O'Brien!'

I waited patiently for her to finish, delighting in the flow of words from her rich Irish tongue. She was, perhaps, about forty, but could have been twenty-five when she smiled. Her short, plump figure sagged and bulged, and she obviously wore no corset. Her apron was soiled, and her feet encased in old felt slippers. She was slovenly and probably quite unsuited to housekeeping, but there was something appealing about her that I instantly recognised—a warm, compassionate, comfortable woman. A baby girl sat on her hip eating a bar of chocolate, and it was plastered freely over her face. Her legs and hands were blue in the biting east wind cutting across the square.

The front door opened onto a passage. The wallpaper had a drab pattern of ivy leaves and the staircase at the end of the passage was covered with shabby carpet, frayed at the edges. All was unutterably dreary, and a strong smell of fried onions pervaded the house. The telephone rang as we stood together in the passage, both holding a heavy suitcase.

'Mother of God!' exclaimed Mrs O'Brien, with fresh indignation. 'Is there no peace at all, at all?'

She dropped my case, perched the baby on the hall-stand, and lifted the receiver. Her voice was melting Irish honey, and she chatted for some ten minutes, on the tenants, the rents, the vacant rooms and the state of the second-floor bathroom. The baby wriggled uncomfortably on her bare buttocks, and beat her mother's face with a sticky fist. Slamming down the receiver, Mrs O'Brien explained.

'It was Mr Harvey, telephoning from Torquay, he what owns this house, the miserable old miser! 'Tis impossible to playse him now, and I could be working me fingers to the bone, and only one pound a week does he pay me, and the bed-sitting room in the basement rent free, and for nothing.' She picked up the case, and I followed her up the stairs. She continued the story as we climbed, breathlessly, to the top landing. 'But I've got me own front door in the back yard. What more could a woman be asking than her own front door?' She tossed the question over her shoulder.

'Number Eight' was a small back room with sloping ceilings, and Mrs O'Brien flicked at a cobweb with a yellow duster she carried in the pocket of her apron. The room contained an iron bedstead, draped in a white quilt, a small wardrobe, a sagging armchair, a dressing table with a cracked mirror, a strip of threadbare matting, a gas-fire and gas-ring with a meter for shillings, and an orange-box cupboard, containing an odd assortment of plates, cups and saucers, cutlery, a tin kettle and a frying pan. A hideous vase had a place of honour on the mantelpiece.

''Tis a fine view from the window, m'dear,' said Mrs O'Brien, determined to point out the assets rather than the defects of Number Eight.

It was indeed a fine view, for it looked down on the trees in the square, and a half acre of grass bordered by a hedge of laurel. The trees were splendid in their autumn glory, with the sun filtering through the tinted leaves.

I pushed up the window and leaned out. Yes, I could manage to live here quite happily, and I could 'make do' with the rather dingy little attic room. Here were the trees!

'There's a fine new wash-basin and a line for your washing and the bathroom on the next floor down. You couldn't be finding anything better now, m'dear, for fifteen shillings a week,' the rich Irish voice reminded me.

'I'm sure I couldn't, but this is perfect. I did so hope it would be on the top floor. It's quieter, you see—I'm a writer, and I'm going to write my first novel here.'

Her eyes widened, and she seemed most impressed.

'Holy Mary! But that's a fine way to make a living now. 'Tis the best room in the whole house for quietness. The girls in Seven and Nine will be out all day and half the night, but 'tis none of my business, and I'll not be enquiring into their private affairs.'

She offered to give me some milk for tea so I followed her down to the basement room where she lived with the child. Was she a widow? She wore no wedding ring and did not mention a husband. A gas-fire blazed in the dirty hearth. It was suffocatingly hot. The cluttered table had not been cleared from the last meal, and a half-eaten sausage was stuck to the plate in a rim of grease.

'It's very warm in here,' I panted.

She threw me a mischievous glance, and dumped the child on the floor.

'One pound a week wages and free room with gas. Why should I be turning if off, when I haven't to put the shillings in the meter?'

She offered me the milk bottle on the table. Only the cream had been taken from the top to garnish a mashed banana on a saucer, which the child had apparently discarded in favour of a currant bun. She insisted that I take it all and waived my offer of payment. With renewed thanks I escaped from the room and ran upstairs, for here, in my own little attic, I could savour the start of a new chapter of my life.

It was a challenge, this adventure into unexplored places and the new experience of a London apartment house. Mrs O'Brien had told me we were a mixed bunch of tenants, as we went downstairs together. A retired Colonel, with a Siamese cat, a middle-aged spinster, a young Welsh student at the London School of Music, a professor from Prague, two Austrian refugees, the three girls, who were shorthand typists, and a Polish widow. A mixed bunch indeed, but good material for a budding novelist, I decided, as I brewed my first pot of tea. Then I settled down to write.

*   *   *   *   *

In two months I had written thousands of words, and torn up more than half. I was left with only six chapters. It was a laborious and lonely business.

There could be only one hero for my first novel—a tall, distinguished man, with searching dark eyes, a naval officer! He was a character drawn from my own unhappy experience, yet he had no life of his own but was merely a puppet, speaking the words I put into his mouth. I sought desperately for the essence and depth of his character. I tried to recall his voice, but that too had escaped. I gave him a family, a college education, and a sweetheart. They all obediently acted their parts, but they too were puppets. The tenants in the apartment house were real, live, interesting and absorbing characters, but the characters I invented were made of card-board.

I had bumped into young David Jenkins one afternoon during my first week at the apartment house, as he stumbled down the dark passage from his own little back room, on the ground floor. He was a stocky, sandy-haired youth, who blushed like a girl, and moved clumsily. He looked like a country-bred boy, and not in the least like a brilliant pianist. Yet, according to Mrs O'Brien, who was mothering him, he had won a three year scholarship at the London School of Music.

'Hullo—you must be David?'

He muttered an apology for nearly tripping me up.

'I heard you practising in the sitting-room yesterday. It must be wonderful to be able to play like that. I tried myself, once-upon-a-time, but discovered I had no talent at all,' I confessed.

'But, Mrs O'Brien tells me you are writing a book, I call that clever. I've never met a writer before.' He sang his words rather than spoke them, for he came from a mining village in the Rhondda Valley.

'Are you just off to the College now?'

'No, I'm going for a walk in the park to freshen up.'

'So am I, for the same reason—shall we go together?'

He grinned boyishly.

'It will be company.'

I discovered during that walk together that he was having rather a struggle to manage on his grant, and often spent the evening in Mrs O'Brien's basement room, when he ran out of shillings for the meter. He also confessed to being homesick.

'Sunday is an awful long day, when the College is closed. After I've been to Chapel in the morning, I'm bored to death, sure to goodness,' he sighed.

'But surely you meet other Welsh people at Chapel. Wouldn't they invite you to their homes if they knew you were lonely?'

'Possibly I come away too quickly.'

I supposed that he was either too shy or too proud to accept hospitality he could not afford to return. His mouth was stubborn, and it would not be easy to persuade him against his will.

'But you *are* glad about the scholarship?'

'Glad? I just couldn't believe it. It was the biggest surprise of my whole life.'

I heard a tremor in that singing voice, and he turned his head away to hide the emotion the memory had rekindled. His big, blunt-fingered hands were thrust into his trouser pockets. Looking at those hands I would have supposed he was a labourer. What an extraordinary talent, and where did it come from?

'Do you come from a musical family?' I wanted to know.

'Only the singing, but everyone sings in Wales. My father is a miner and he sings in the Chapel choir. It was my mother who encouraged me to play the piano when I was only a little bit of a lad. She took in washing to pay for my music lessons. It is my mother who sends me pocket money, not very much, but it's all she can manage. Mark you, when it's gone, I have to do without any. It's not difficult, I've never had very much anyway.'

'That makes two of us, David, I also have a wonderful mother, but we have been 'making do' all our lives!'

He wanted to know about my family, my home, my village. It was like having Jock, the Seventh Engineer, all over again. But he wasn't in the least like Jock in other respects, for he lived and breathed music. It was his only love. He talked of Beethoven and Brahms with an easy familiarity, but stumbled over such elementary subjects as nature study. He confessed to an appalling ignorance of birds and trees and flowers, and could not distinguish a beech from a birch, or a celandine from a buttercup! He had never even noticed the changing seasons of the year, and this, to me, was quite inconceivable, yet completely honest.

He agreed with me about the talents, though—that they were born in one, and should be developed, not wasted. His views were often compatible with mine, although he was ten years younger. After a long bracing walk in the park, we would sit in a Lyons tea-shop, enjoying a cup of tea and a bun. Sometimes he allowed me to pay for this but not often. When his turn came for two free tickets to a concert of classical music, at the Queen's Hall, he invited me to join him.

'But I'm not a highbrow! I shan't know whether it's a symphony or a concerto, a Schumann or a Chopin!' I confessed.

His shaggy eyebrows twitched. He was trying not to laugh.

'You see what I mean about the beech and the birch? One can't be an authority on everything!' he teased.

But I did enjoy the concert, particularly the two works of

Chopin—the Impromptu No 2 in F Sharp Major and the Ballade No 1 in G Minor. Tchaikovsky's First Piano Concerto, I *did* recognise, for it was an old favourite since my fifteenth year, when I spent a month in a Convalescent Home in Surrey and listened entranced to a recording.

'I've just had an idea,' said David, over the tea cups in Lyons one afternoon in early December, 'Why don't you write a lyric, and I could set it to music?'

'Could you?'

'Well, I could try,' he corrected, with his customary modesty.

That same evening I wrote the lyric and left it with him before he went to the College the following morning.

Later in the day, as I hurried out to collect some shopping, he called me into the sitting-room.

'Listen to this. Tell me if you like it.'

He played over a rather melancholy little tune that seemed to fit the words of the lyric perfectly.

'I like it, David. Play it again.'

We liked it so much we composed several more, and David copied out the scores. It kept him amused on wet Sundays, and he had no time to be bored. Now we fancied ourselves as professional song-writers, and I trudged around all the music publishers in 'Tin Pan Alley,' with copies of our masterpieces, and wild hopes of making an easy fortune!

'Not commercially marketable,' they all said to me, but we laughed a lot over this episode, and remained as poor as church mice for the rest of our stay at the apartment house.

*　　*　　*　　*　　*

The front door opened slowly one winter afternoon, and a slight bearded figure carefully closed his umbrella.

'Now, Professor, haven't I told you I would be after changing the library books when I'd finished with the cleaning?' Mrs O'Brien scolded, and flicked off the raindrops with the bright yellow duster.

She loved the way he removed his hat on entering the house, and held it pressed to his chest like a shield. It gave her a pleasant feeling of being a lady in her own right. The child, who had taken an immediate liking to the old gentleman on his arrival from Prague, six months ago, smiled her gaping, toothless smile, and stretched her arms towards him.

'Yes, my little one, I take you, but first I remove the damp overcoat. Zo!'

With the coat and hat on the hallstand, and the books tucked under one arm, he took the child on the other, and climbed the stairs slowly, for the small, throttling arms around his neck made his breathing heavy and laboured. Mrs O'Brien had hastily covered the child's bare buttocks with the yellow duster, to save embarrassment, and she watched his careful progress with mixed feelings. Would he keep the child long enough for a quick dash to the pastry shop in Westbourne Grove, or would he want to hand her back after giving her a chocolate? As if in answer to these unspoken questions, the Professor leaned over the banisters, and gasped, breathlessly,

'I keep her till four o'clock. It is no trouble.'

Calling the blessings of Saint Patrick on the kind old gentleman, Mrs O'Brien plunged happily down the basement stairs.

Papa and Mama Zolamek, who lived in the front bed-sitting room on the same landing, heard the Professor talking to the child, but kept their door closed. They could not bear to look at her, and her crying stirred such poignant memories in them that it seemed they would be better dead than living this way, in their adopted country.

Mama was huddled, as usual, over the gas-fire. She, who once had been the dominant partner, was now dependent as a child. It was her strange, unnatural passiveness that made life so difficult now for poor Papa Zolamek, for he had now to shoulder the entire responsibility of their rehabilitation. Although they had met with so much kindness, he was still confused and stunned by the appalling discoveries of the past twelve months. His mind had refused to believe it had happened, but the emptiness of his heart and his wife's condition were sufficient proof.

Their three children—Joseph, Rachel and Benjamin—had disappeared as mysteriously as the neighbours they had known all their married life. The children, on their way to school, had turned at the corner of the street to wave to their parents standing in the doorway of their little patisserie—and then they had vanished. Months of frantic enquiries had brought no definite information, but vague rumours that they had been seen getting into a car in the market square at Salzburg. But Salzburg was thirty miles away, and they had no relatives there—only an old acquaintance of their father's they had not seen since he became an active member of the new Nazi Party. Party politics had never concerned Papa Zolamek. He was a family man and a pastry cook, and not at all clever, compared to his wife, who had been a school teacher before her marriage. All three children had their mother's looks and intelligence, and Papa was inordinately proud of them.

The language barrier prevented any real contact with them, but Mrs O'Brien had passed on the bare facts of their pitiful story to the rest of the tenants.

At the landlord's suggestion, she kept the first floor rooms for the 'foreigners' which seemed to segregate them from the rest. The pungent smell of freshly brewed coffee hung over this landing, and I often caught a glimpse of a short, stout little man, with a balding head, emptying a bucket of slops into the lavatory.

Colonel Fraser, and his Siamese cat, Mia, occupied the best front room, on the ground floor. He paid the princely sum of thirty shillings weekly rent, for this privilege, but it included service, and a small kitchen.

The Colonel was tall, grey-haired and distinguished. Mrs O'Brien was much in awe of him and hovered on the basement stairs till he was safely out of the house, when she rushed in to make his bed, and clean the room. Fortunately, his movements were so regular, she knew exactly when he would be out or in, and he never left Mia for more than an hour. He told nobody his business and was a law unto himself.

During the two years he had lived at the apartment house he had received few letters and no visitors. But he was a great reader, and brought back an armful of books from the Public Library every week. We sometimes saw him in the distance— David and I—when we walked in the park, striding along in true military style, seeing nothing and nobody but the way ahead.

Mia was his constant companion and he talked to her as an equal. They had the same dignity, and the same disdain. I thought they were admirably suited to each other. Mia would sit erect as a statue on the Colonel's armchair, and watch every flick of the bright, yellow duster with inscrutable blue eyes.

'Mercy of God!' Mrs O'Brien would exclaim nervously, as

she gathered up the mats; the child would be left to crawl on the floor in the passage, for she was terrified of Mia.

Between the Colonel's room and David's little back room was another bed-sitting room, usually locked, for Miss Ursula Bennet also discouraged friendly overtures, and had no need of the housekeeper's services, for she cleaned her own room, and had her lunch at a rather exclusive little restaurant in Queensway. Her main interest in life was the Church, and she devoted many hours every week to helping the Vicar with parish affairs, hospital visiting and Sunday School. Like the Colonel, Miss Bennet disclosed nothing at all concerning her family, her background, or her past. She might have been any age between forty and sixty—a tall, gaunt figure, neatly but severely dressed in drab colours, and invariably wearing a felt hat and carrying an umbrella. She had, however, one distinguishing feature which saved her face from plainness—remarkable dark eyes of deep intensity. I suspected, from the beginning, that she had a secret passion for the Colonel, and was jealous of Mia, but the rest of the tenants she ignored.

The other tenant, on the 'foreigners' floor', was a widow, with an unpronounceable name, from an unpronounceable place in Poland. She worked long hours as a chambermaid in a Bloomsbury hotel, and spent her free days in bed.

To me, the other tenants were curiously fascinating, with their varied individual lives, and their complete disregard of each other, for they seemed to have nothing in common.

Behind the closed doors of seven bed-sitting rooms, Mrs O'Brien's tenants heard the declaration of war, one Sunday morning, in September 1939. But the doors remained closed, and I could only try to imagine the feelings, fears and frustration in all these different minds and hearts under the same roof.

Only David and Mrs O'Brien emerged as I ran downstairs. 'That man Hitler—he was a liar, sure to goodness,' said David, dispassionately.

*   *   *   *   *

Mia was surprised to see the Colonel in a tin hat, and her blue eyes were scornful. The word 'Warden' was printed on the front of the tin hat in large white capitals, and it sat on his dignified grey head as incongrously as a mushroom on a beanstalk. A gas mask was slung over his shoulder and he carried a heavy torch.

With this extraordinary new outfit went a complete change of personality. His pallid face flushed with excitement. He looked younger, more animated, and was inclined to swagger. Books were returned to the Public Library, and he was often seen hurrying down the front steps, and striding across the square with a purposeful air, to the ARP post, in a back street near Paddington Station.

'I've been put in charge,' he told Mrs O'Brien proudly.

The war had saved him from a slow, enforced degeneration, and he regarded his new responsibility, with the recruiting and training of volunteers, as a tremendous challenge to his initiative and capabilities.

Encouraged by such a splendid example, Miss Bennet hurried off to the headquarters of the WVS and was enrolled for voluntary service. She looked very neat and efficient in her new green uniform. The Vicar, I imagine, was obliged to find another helper, for she became so involved with the WVS her duties took priority over everything else. I often saw her in the Underground pushing a tea trolley along the crowded platform.

Tiers of bunks had been erected and army blankets provided for the 'squatters' who spent their nights in this improvised Underground air-raid shelter. Papa and Mama Zolamek left the apartment house in mid-afternoon, to make certain of securing two of the bunks. Papa carried a bulging canvas bag with essentials for passing the long hours on the Underground platform, and this included a flask of black coffee, for they found no refreshment in the weak beverage provided by the kind ladies of the WVS. Indeed they were constantly amazed by the British habit of tea-drinking, and the importance attached to it.

They also provided themselves with caraway seed bread, salami sausage, cheese and a few ginger biscuits to dip in the coffee. Mama took her knitting, but seldom did more than a couple of rows, and Papa had the Polish newspaper provided by the refugee organisation. In a little string bag on Mama's arm, her precious treasures were carried, and she slept with the bag pressed to her breast. It contained only three articles—Joseph's Hebrew bible, Rachel's little tasselled cap, and Benjamin's red slippers.

The dusty laurels in the centre of the square had been hacked down by Council workmen, and several Anderson shelters provided for those residents who were too nervous to sleep in their own houses and too fastidious to share the crowded platforms of the Underground. Gangs of workmen were digging air-raid shelters in the parks, and barrage balloons drifted overhead, like enormous fat whales. Everyone expected the German Luftwaffe to launch an attack at any hour of the day or night. Every man, woman and child carried a gas mask as part of their equipment, all through the autumn and winter of 1939. All unmarried women between the age of 18 and 40 registered at the Ministry of Labour.

I was directed to County Hall as a 'third grade clerical assistant', at a salary that barely covered my lodgings, food and fares to Westminster.

Reporting for duty, one Monday morning, I realised with sudden alarming clarity, that I was no longer an individual, but a number in a register, and that I was no longer free to choose. I had lost my identity. For the duration of the war I would be compelled to conform to the standards and demands of the Ministry—to go where I was sent, to obey instructions.

It was a solemn and rather frightening moment when this thought struck me. I was walking briskly across Westminster Bridge in a stream of pedestrians. The river flowed quietly beneath our hurrying feet, the urgency of our business unreflected in the dark waters. A barge, piled with timber slid under the bridge, in the wake of a small motor launch. I envied both the river pilot and the bargee, for they seemed to be still enjoying a measure of independent movement that the rest of us were denied. But this may have been an illusion, and they were probably restricted to certain channels on the river, for the duration of the war.

So I joined the queue of new recruits in the main lobby, to present my card of introduction and to await instructions. The polished corridors echoed to the tramp of feet, and the wide stairways were blocked with a solid mass of men and women, propelled upwards, by force of habit and necessity, to the rows of offices, each clearly labelled with its own identification number.

The office manager of S73 passed a cursory glance over the

fresh contingent—four very ordinary-looking women, with little to recommend them, but a certain eagerness to get started.

'The sooner we start, the sooner we get finished,' said one, philosophically.

His wan smile at this remark, included me, the youngest, and we were invited to sit down and relax, until such time as he could attend to us. We could do our knitting if we wished, and find our way to the Canteen, later, for the coffee break. He apologised for having no work on hand, but he hadn't expected us. Every department was being compelled to accept untrained personnel, and the Ministry of Labour was to blame for this ridiculous situation, he explained.

The hours dragged. I had no knitting, and my sighs and fidgeting seemed to annoy the older women, who had come prepared with wool, needles and patterns, and were quite happily waiting, now the situation had been explained to them. Several young men sat at their desks absorbed in the piles of documents, bank notes and invoices, all relating to the expenditure involved in the mass evacuation of children.

When I was almost ready to scream from sheer boredom, the manager suggested we go to lunch.

'Don't hurry back, take your time,' we were told.

So I wandered along the Embankment, and sat down on the low stone parapet overlooking the river, to eat my sandwiches and apple; oppressed by the awful tediousness of my first day in this new environment, and the certain conviction of being a square peg in a round hole!

*   *   *   *   *

David had been enrolled in a fire-watching team of local residents, and spent two nights a week walking round the area. He was also given a tin hat, and a torch with a blue reflector, and he had some amusing stories to tell of absent-minded ladies who forgot to pull the black-out curtains before switching on all the lights.

Our Sunday walks in the park gave us both an opportunity to relax from our war-time obligations, and discuss the topics in which we were both interested. But already he was torn between two conflicting loyalties—to his mother and the sponsors of the scholarship, and to his country. Senior students were leaving the college every week to join the Services and I found him moody and depressed on our last walk together, the week before the end of term.

'I'm not coming back, I've signed on for the Merchant Navy,' he told me, quietly, over a plate of toast in the Lyons tea-shop.

I could have wept for him.

'It seems such a waste, David, couldn't you finish out your last year? Nobody expects you to join up. After all, you are still a student.'

His eyes met mine across the table, and suddenly I realised he was no longer a boy. The powerful hands, with their blunt fingers, were spread on the table, and he looked at them without speaking; his mouth set stubbornly. His hands had always fascinated me, for they were the hands of a manual worker, not a professional pianist. All his features were blunt, without any refinement. But when he sat down to play, he was instantly transformed, and his ugliness was no longer noticed. The beauty and brilliance of his performance, when interpreting the old masters, left one in no doubt of his great talents.

For me, that last Sunday evening, he played my favourite Chopin Preludes. Tears pricked my eyes, and my throat tightened with sadness for this was the end of another chapter, and another friendship. The other tenants were still withdrawn and difficult to know, but David had seemed like a younger brother. I would miss him and his music more than I yet realised.

Three months later, Mrs O'Brien received a letter from his mother saying that the tanker on which David had been travelling in convoy, en route to the Balkans, had been torpedoed. There were no survivors.

*   *   *   *   *

That first Christmas of the war was spent at home with Mother and her two small evacuees from Lambeth.

All the rest of the family were away. William had left the branch bank where he had been employed for some years and now he was training at an Army Officers' Camp, somewhere in the West Country. Henry was working in munitions and

Mary had been put in charge of a day nursery at Brighton. Jackie had joined his first ship at the age of sixteen.

Mother was completely absorbed in these two evacuees—a brother and sister, aged four and six—and quite unconcerned about the war.

Last year's Christmas tree was dug up from the garden, and the children helped me to decorate it with the coloured balls, bells, tinsel, and fairy doll, that Henry had packed carefully away in the loft. We also found paper-chains, silver stars, and the manger Henry had made for Jackie as a little boy. The figures of Mary and Joseph and the Baby were battered and crumbling. The cattle had lost their tails, and the shepherds had each lost a leg, but the children received them rapturously. The manger was assembled to the strains of an old recording of 'Swanee River' and 'Old Father Thames'.

The evacuees had brought their toy gramophone and a splendid selection of records, for they liked a background of noise, even when we played Snap and Happy Families. They had no Nursery Rhyme records and thought they were 'soppy'. They had no use for cuddles and kisses either, I soon discovered. Mother's attitude was exactly right for them, for she had never indulged in 'dears' and 'darlings', was sensible, matter-of-fact, and unemotional.

'She lets us 'elp ourselves. We don't never 'ave our jam spread, Miss,' the boy reminded me at tea time, that first day. And when I had apologised, his four-year-old sister added pertly, 'We 'as our own proper knives too, and don't eat noffink wiv a spoon, so there!'

*   *   *   *   *

With Christmas over, I began a long persistent campaign to join the WRNS. The 'Wrens' were considered the elite of the Women's Services, but I had not realised the high standard of education and physical fitness required of every new recruit.

I haunted the London Headquarters, wrote letters to the Commanding Officers, filled up questionnaires, and actually succeeded in passing the theory and oral tests—as a 'rating' of course! Officer standards were much higher and degrees or diplomas expected. Nevertheless, I should enjoy life as a 'rating' and the uniform, with its pert little sailor hat would suit me nicely!

Bored to distraction at County Hall, I passed my days in hurrying along corridors with sheaves of papers to X130, P54 or T250, in search of information for my long-suffering departmental manager. I was convinced he was only sending me on these fruitless journeys to get me out of the office, for he was weary of my demands for 'something to do.' The young men had been drafted elsewhere, and the four women had each acquired a desk, a clean blotter and a drawer in which to keep cosmetics and knitting—I had neither! But I was entrusted with the checking and balancing of piles of bank pass books. The reason for this escaped me during the whole of the three months I was engaged on this task, for it seemed as pointless and time-wasting as the search for non-existent information in the files.

Then, one day, I was allowed time off to attend a medical examination at the WRNS headquarters, which decided, completely and finally my *un*fitness for the Services. The naval doctor regarded my badly scarred stomach with interest and amusement.

'Sorry, old girl—one hundered per cent fitness for the Wrens, I'm afraid, *not* ninety-nine and three quarters!'

Mother had suggested that I enrol in the Women's Land Army, to get me out of London, and back to the country where I rightly belonged. But the few girls I had met in breeches and boots had been strong, sturdy types, with plenty of muscle for pushing heavy wheelbarrows, and mucking out stables. So I now had to face the fact that I had no choice but to remain a civilian for the duration of the war.

But why should I stay at County Hall. Why not apply for a transfer?

For the second time I joined the queue at the Ministry of Labour.

The counter clerk gave me a cold stare of disapproval as I hurriedly explained my business.

'There's a war on,' he informed me, curtly, 'we have no time for dealing with dissatisfied people,'

'But I am only dissatisfied because I haven't enough to do. There must be a useful job I could do somewhere, surely?'

Sighing with exasperation he flicked over the documents on the counter.

'I'll transfer you to the Ministry of Aircraft Production. Report there on February 1.'

'Thank you! Thank you very much!'

His mouth twitched, and I thought he was going to laugh.

'You will still be a Grade Three Clerical Officer, so one place is as good as another,' he reminded me.

He was right. There was no sense of urgency in the new Ministry, either. The foyer reminded me of a West End hotel, and the Commissionaire, in his smart uniform, rather like a head porter. One expected to meet the guests in the lift, or a page-boy in the corridor. The atmosphere was informal and friendly. Senior personnel seemed to be engaged in interminable 'conferences' in boardrooms smelling deliciously of whisky and cigars.

I was immediately shuttled into an office, and told to wait for an indefinite period, with nothing to do but sigh. My 'potential' was assessed for the first week, and it was decided I could join a rather select company of 'Grade Threes' engaged on work of great secrecy—or so they said. It seemed unlikely that inexperienced women clerks would be entrusted with anything of real importance! Yet it boosted the morale tremendously to be invited to join this select company of twelve in a big office filled with filing cabinets, in which were stored blueprints and documents referring to all our main aircraft factories.

I was allocated the cabinet marked Westhill Aircraft Company, Somerset. Was it Fate or mere coincidence, that I should be allocated the one place in the British Isles where I was destined to meet the man I should love so devastatingly? I still cannot believe it was mere Chance. Surely there must be a pattern, a design, in living and loving?

But I had no premonition of such a meeting at the time.

* * * * *

'I have nothing to offer you but BLOOD, TOIL, TEARS AND SWEAT.'

The compelling voice of Winston Churchill caught Mrs O'Brien patching a broken window pane with the lid of a shoe box.

'That's nothing fresh now, for I've had it all me life!' she told the child irritably.

The apartment house was in a most depressing state these days, with plaster falling from the ceilings every time the house was shaken by bomb blasts, smashed windows, and a heap of rubble in the backyard. The front steps were permanently covered with a thick layer of dust and crumbled cement. Mrs O'Brien constantly threatened to give notice, and declared the place was getting more like Waterloo Station every day!

A thin marmalade cat trod delicately over a pile of broken tiles as she dragged the push-cart up the area steps, one Sunday afternoon, with the child tucked under her arm. They were on their way to St Joseph's, for four o'clock Mass, and when they had fulfilled their duty to the church and Father Donovan, they would hurry back to Westbourne Grove, to see the Sunday film at the Roxy. Sunday was the happiest day of the week for them—their only free day. The mother, who was as young in heart as the child, was just as easily amused, delighted, or upset. When one cried, the other wept in sympathy, and tears flowed copiously during these emotional days of 1940.

The postman and the milkman would both tell harrowing tales over the tea-cups in the basement room. Tales of blitzed homes, and bodies buried under the rubble, while Mrs O'Brien listened enthralled with tears streaming down her cheeks. In a morbid sense, she enjoyed hearing and repeating all the grue-some details, and often took the child in the push-cart in the afternoon to inspect the damage in the streets around the square. They met other regular sightseers to the ruins, and when an area was cordoned off by the police because of the danger of an unexploded bomb, a crowd gathered to stare at the site and speculate on the damage that could have been done had it exploded as Hitler intended. His name was bandied as freely now as a household word, and the few children who were left in the area played games in which the central figure was curiously like Charlie Chaplin. Many of the children were brought back from the first evacuation, after a few months of the 'phoney war', but hurriedly sent away again in the spring of 1940.

The majority of these children were not seen again for several years, and some preferred to stay with their adopted families, especially in the Welsh mining villages, where they learned to speak the language at school, became a part of the community, and settled down happily. The few children who were left behind were either too young, or too homesick to be evacuated, and I would see them on their way to the Anderson air-raid shelters in the square, with mothers and grandmothers, dogs, cats and budgerigars, toys and books. Enid Blyton was the popular children's author, and her little books were seen everywhere. No child would dream of spending the night in the shelter without an Enid Blyton.

Magazines had almost disappeared from the bookstalls, and newspapers limited to small editions, printed on poor quality paper. The wireless was the centre of family entertainment and information, and many sets were left switched on all day, for the frequent news bulletins.

Mrs O'Brien switched on automatically as she drank her early morning tea, and switched off before she climbed into bed, after the nine o'clock news. It was 'company' she told me. The strains of Sandy McPherson's organ followed her up the basement stairs, for he obligingly filled in all gaps in the BBC programmes and acquired a vast unseen audience all over the country. 'Itma' was another regular feature, with Tommy Handley and 'Mrs Mopp', asking plaintively, 'Can I do you *now*, Sir?' The rhythm of Jack Payne and his dance band beat incessantly from the open windows of clubs, cafés and dance halls, and we would all learn to sing the new songs that were as catching as the songs of the First World War. 'Roll out the barrow', 'There'll always be an England', 'We joined the navy to see the world', 'There'll be bluebirds over the white cliffs of Dover' and 'Run Rabbit, Run Rabbit, Run! Run! Run!'. Dr Malcolm Sargent was a prominent figure now, since he continued to conduct his Sunday night concerts in the Queen's Hall until it was bombed.

After David left, I attended only one more concert, but came out during the interval. The programme included his favourite Rachmaninov Second Piano Concerto, and I could not bear to hear it. That was the night I spent in the vaults of the YMCA in Tottenham Court Road, because of a heavy raid. For a shilling I was provided with a camp bed and an army blanket, and joined the rows of 'squatters' for a lively and amusing night.

Some families were camping there permanently for the duration of the war, many were homeless, and some, like myself, caught on the pavement as the sirens wailed their warning. In a corner near my bed a young mother was quietly reading *Winnie the Pooh* to her three-year-old son, and then she heard his prayers. The lavatory walls were plastered with rude drawings of Hitler, Goering and Goebbels. But the ladies of the WVS, pushing their tea-trolley through the crowded vaults, still managed to maintain an air of garden-party decorum in their neat green uniforms.

Then I saw the Professor, leaning against the wall, calmly reading his Bible, surrounded by a family of refugees.

At six o'clock the next morning I was served with a breakfast of bacon and eggs, toast and coffee, at Lyons Corner House. Never had a breakfast tasted so good, or coffee smelt so delicious!

The Wardens coming off duty, after the 'All Clear' Siren, looked grey and exhausted, but the savoury breakfast smells brought the cheerful grins back to their lined faces.

'Thank God for Joe Lyon!' said a grey-haired veteran of the First World War gratefully.

$$* \quad * \quad * \quad * \quad *$$

The sky was still red with the flames of burning warehouses, and the stench of smouldering wood still in his nostrils, as the Colonel walked wearily back across the square, after another long night on duty. He was driving himself too hard these days, and often volunteered for extra duty when one of his men reported sick, or had some kind of domestic trouble.

Poor old 'Pop', a veteran of the last war had lost his wife in one of those senseless raids on the suburbs. Barney's son had been shot down in a Spitfire over the Channel, and Bill Mercer, who was in charge of the Rescue Squad, was still waiting for news of his boy, Richard, reported missing nine months ago from a mine-sweeper in the North Sea.

Bill was a big, blustering fellow, but he wasn't ashamed to be seen weeping. The Colonel wished he could rid himself of pent-up feelings with the same easy and childlike abandon. And it must be quite a relief, he thought enviously, to stand up and bellow—'Bastards! Bloody bastards!'—or to let the scalding tears stream unashamedly down your face, instead of choking them back in your throat. But it was all a matter of early training and environment, of disciplined self-control and a stern sense of right and wrong. The pattern of his life had been black and white, ordered and regulated, not haphazard. The Army had been his whole life, his career, and his one absorbing passion. He had never married, or felt the need of wife and children, for his mother had presided over his house, relieved him of all domestic worries and adored him!

After her death, in 1935, and his retirement from the Army the following year, he moved into his London club, but decided, two years later, he couldn't afford it. Still keeping his membership and enjoying its amenities, he went in search of rooms among the many new apartment houses in the squares within walking distance of Hyde Park.

The square that he finally decided on still had a certain dignity and Georgian elegance. It was quiet, and he saw no children playing in the street. But soon the aspect and atmospere had completely changed. There were prams on the front steps, motor-bikes roared past the house late into the night, and radio sets blared out popular tunes. A new era had started, an era of bed-sitting rooms. The small enclosed garden, with its hedge of laurels and flowering shrubs, where once the private tenants of the square had exercised their dogs, finally disappeared beneath the bricks and mortar of the Anderson shelters. Front steps were dirty, door knobs unpolished, and rubble piled in the basement yards. When the Colonel was tired—and who wasn't tired these days—he was depressed by this general neglect in the square, by the dirt and dust, and the stray, mongrel cats prowling around the pavements. They had survived, while his adored Mia had disappeared into thin air. Nothing made sense any more. As he pushed open the door of his room his eyes travelled automatically to his armchair, where he still expected to find her sitting like a small, oriental statue, carved in dignity.

On this particular morning, following a night of heavy bombardment in the Paddington area, the Colonel was feeling dazed and sick, and he could think of nothing but bath and bed. Two of his men had not reported for duty, so he himself had joined the Rescue Squad for the first time, leaving the girl in charge of the Post. It had been a gruesome and horrifying experience. As an Army man he felt outraged that civilians should be sharing the front line of attack. Too tired and nauseated to bother with a meal, he slipped into the bathroom, and stretching his aching limbs in the hot water, he tried to relax. It was the only luxury he indulged in, and the house-keeper, though pretty hopeless as regards cleaning, had always managed to keep the boiler going in the basement. Actually a daily bath was not a luxury for him, but a habit and neces-sity. Slipping into a dressing gown, he lay on the bed, lit a cigarette and closed his eyes.

But for once his disciplined mind was unable to close the door on all disturbing thoughts. It buzzed and hummed with mental pictures of the poor, distorted bodies his men had lifted so gently out of the ruins. With Mia curled in his arms it might have been possible to banish all these night-mares, but now he had to fight them alone.

He still missed her intolerably.

The first to be lifted out had been the little dressmaker, Miss Sims. She had lived in one of a row of terraced houses all her life, and was said to be in her sixties. Bill Mercer had handed her up from the gaping hole, to Barney, who was standing on the edge of the crumbling crater. She had been pinned by the legs for several hours, and had died before they could reach her. Fresh in the Colonel's memory was the sound of her thin voice calling back to her rescuers, as they desperately sought a way to reach her. Then, growing per-ceptively weaker, it had stopped, only a few minutes before two of his men had tunnelled a passage under the girders. She was still wearing her thimble, and a frayed tape-measure hung round her neck.

Perhaps, because she was the first he had actually seen taken out of the ruins, he remembered her most vividly, or perhaps it was Barney's tortured face, in the light of the torch. He had looked like a man on the verge of collapse, yet he stayed with the team all night.

'It's the little people all the time, Chief—the nice, ordinary, little people like this lot in the terrace, that get a blasted packet,' he told the Colonel, as he wiped the sweat from his grimed face, 'God! but it's a damn, lunatic war!'

Six of the houses had disintegrated like a child's castle of bricks, and the rest were hanging open—the walls split from roof to cellar, doors flung into the gardens, but fireplaces still intact in the roofless bedrooms. Furniture hung suspended on broken beams, and a grandfather clock still upright, and still ticking, was the only object left untouched in Number Seven.

They had arrived on the scene a few minutes after the explosions had rocked the Post, and heard, above the roar of crumbling walls and shattering glass a single, terrified scream, then silence—a strange, uncanny silence. They had searched for survivors at the north end of the terrace first, because it was obvious, at a glance, there would be nobody alive in the south end.

A second team were digging under the stairs of Number Ten, and here they found the body of Harry Blake, the bus driver, and his dog, Toby. His wife and children had been evacuated to the country. The two spinster sisters—Angela and Mary Vines—who kept themselves to themselves—must have been killed instantly by blast. The retired railway clerk and his aged mother were found, some hours later, with the couple in Number Twelve, whom they must have been visiting. All four were lying sprawled in the passage, beneath a mountainous pile of rubble from crumbled ceilings.

Checking on the list of residents, only one was missing as dawn was breaking—Mrs Casey, a widow, whose son was in the Navy.

The two groups of men had been joined by three men and a girl from the AFS and the ambulance was standing by. The girl was handing round mugs of tea, and the men, grimed with dust and dirt, heavy-eyed and exhausted, had gathered round the AFS truck.

A slight, boyish figure, in bell-bottom trousers and a sailor hat, scrambled out of a taxi, with a bulging kit-bag, and ran towards them.

'Where's Mum?' he demanded. He looked no more than seventeen, and his eyes were frightened. Dropping the kit-bag in the rubble, he searched the group of silent men, and his young face blanched and quivered.

'Steady now, take it easy, lad,' Bill Mercer's voice was gruff. 'We haven't given up hope, we'll go on searching till we find her, son.'

He picked up his spade, and the others spread out in a half circle, and began to dig. The boy sat down on a broken doorpost, with his hat still perched at a jaunty angle on the back of his head, and his hands hanging loosely between his knees. The Colonel sat down beside him, and offered him a cigarette. He was not very clever with reassuring speeches, Bill and Barney were better at that sort of thing, but he could be a good listener.

'I came as soon as I could, honest I did,' the boy explained, and blew a cloud of smoke into the air. 'We only docked last night. They told me at Liverpool Street that Paddington had caught another packet, so I hopped in a taxi. I couldn't get here any quicker, Sir, could I?'

But before the Colonel could answer, the last remnants of the boy's self-control seemed to snap, and he jumped up, to run wildly over the heaps of rubble, sobbing and crying.

'Mum! Mum! You must find her! You must!'

Bill Mercer stopped digging, climbed out of the trench, and clasped the slim, shaking shoulders.

'We've found her, son,' he said quietly.

The boy wiped his eyes across his sleeve, and stumbled towards the trench.

'Steady lad, take it easy,' Barney put out a helping hand, but the boy ignored it, and slid down the bank of earth and plaster, to where a slight, aproned figure lay sprawled across a broken mangle.

'Mum! Mum!'

He fell on her, shaking her senseless shoulders.

'Mum! Speak to me!' His voice broke on a long wail of hopelessness. 'Speak to me, Mum *please*!' Folding her in his arms, he turned savagely on the group of waiting, silent men. 'Do something then! Don't just stand there! Blast you! It's Mum, it's her alright.' And his strong young arms tightened around the limp figure.

'I'm sorry, son, we did our best,' said Bill, humbly, but the boy was not listening. He was stroking the poor bruised face, and plastered hair.

'You mustn't get mad at me, Mum, I came as soon as I could,' he was explaining in a small frightened voice.

Once more the ambulance slid over the scattered heaps of rubble, and a stretcher party stepped carefully over a pile of bricks.

'She'll be alright, won't she?' he asked, tentatively, as they loosened his frantic hold and gently covered the little figure with a blanket.

'Yes, she'll be alright, we'll take good care of her.'

Barney's pinched face quivered and Bill let out a single explosive 'Bastards!' But it was the girl from the AFS who showed the most resourcefulness.

'You'd better come home with me, kid,' she said, casually, leaning out of the driver's seat.

And the young sailor picked up his kit-bag and climbed in beside her, without a backward glance.

* * * * * *

Ursula Bennet had spent all day on that Sunday in June 1940 listening to the Colonel calling his cat, Mia.

It was the first free Sunday they had enjoyed for three months, and it should have been spent in a sensible way, sitting quietly in the park, or taking a walk in the fresh air— separately, of course, for the Colonel had never once suggested they walk together. Ursula had almost given up hope of getting beyond the stage of passing the time of day, enquiring after Mia's health and the Colonel's activities at the ARP Post. He became quite animated during these short conversations on the front doorstep, but he did not ask her about her own war-effort with the tea-trolley on the Underground, in that stifling atmosphere.

Her nerves were now beginning to crack under the strain. She had imagined, when the war was declared, and they both immediately offered their services, that their brief acquaintance would ripen into friendship. They would have a common bond of sympathy and sacrifice. After all, it had been his ardent enthusiasm in the first place that had sent her hurrying off to register for voluntary service with the WVS. The green uniform was neat and becoming to her tall, sparse figure, and she knew her manner and appearance was not lacking in refinement— 'ladylike' was the word she used. Her only consolation for his total lack of interest was the certainty that she had no rivals for the Colonel's affections in the apartment house. Not one of them could be called 'ladylike', or refined, and her general opinion of the tenants was poor.

'Mia! Mia! Mia!'

She covered her ears with hands that trembled. Would he never stop calling for the cat—or pacing up and down the passage, in and out of the front door, like a man possessed?

Then a small, satisfied smile played over her prim mouth, and her eyes held a gleam of triumph. For she knew.

The hateful creature was dead!

She had watched it die, three days ago, on the sloping roof beneath her window, and made no effort to save it. If she had opened her window when the first trickle of broken bricks and mortar slithered off the chimney, the cat would have rushed inside, scared, but unhurt. But she kept her window closed till it slid over the edge in an avalanche of rubble. Now she kept her eyes averted from the window, for when she glanced that way she saw the cat's supercilious stare, and the small erect figure, still untouched, on the roof.

But why hadn't the Colonel searched the heap of rubble in the yard when he had searched every inch of the house? Had Mrs O'Brien discovered the body and removed it, out of misplaced kindness? These questions still remained unanswered after three days of searching.

They had all helped in the search, even the foreigners, and the girls on the top floor, who seemed quite concerned about the missing cat.

'I shouldn't worry too much, Colonel, if I were you, cats are such independent creatures, and they always come home when they are ready. We once had a ginger cat who was missing for three weeks, then came back with a family of kittens!' laughed Rosemary.

The Colonel shuddered to think of Mia in the same class, but thanked the girls for allowing him to search the cupboards under the eaves.

'Poor old chap, he looks quite cut up,' said Christine, as she finished varnishing her nails.

To Ursula Bennet however, he looked like a man who had received a mortal blow, and she watched him walk across the square, in his tin hat, with shoulders hunched. Now he was more remote than ever, for he avoided her, instead of seeking her company. It was driving her mad.

Then she went to the window, drew aside the black-out curtain and looked out.

The cat was still there!

At that time Rosemary's thoughts were all of Tony. She remembered only the exquisite joy of loving, and being loved, though she had known he was married, that his wife and two young children were living with relatives in Canada, for the war's duration.

Since New Year's Eve when they had accidently collided in a doorway, trying to escape the revellers in Piccadilly Circus, they had met frequently. After that first encounter, and a cup of coffee at the Corner House, they had both known an immediate liking for each other's company, but made no plans to meet again. Medically unfit for the Services at the age of thirty-five, Tony Howes had been drafted to the main postal sorting office in the City, and detailed two nights a week on fire-watching. He was slightly built and quite undistinguised in appearance, but his quietness and gentleness in the midst of so much noise and confusion had a healing, soothing quality that Rosemary found extraordinarily restful. She was lively and talkative, while Tony was restrained, and given to long silences.

Chance had thrown them together on New Year's Eve, and Chance had repeated the strange caprice, in pushing them into the same crowded compartment of an Underground train, a week later. Strap-hanging all the way to Paddington, they had talked over the shoulder of a plump little woman in a dirty head scarf. The sour smell of her sweating armpits mingled with the stale breath of her companion, completely engrossed in the racing results. Tony's pinched face, swaying between the two, was strained and tired, but his eyes were alight with that same gleam of interest and amusement she had seen at their first meeting.

Just back from a week-end at home, she recounted for his benefit the dubious delights of the Saturday night 'hop' at the Village Hall, and her parents' weekly headache with their customers' ration books. As an only child, born to parents near to middle-age, she had been sheltered from infancy in their over-indulgent care. The village stores and post-office was their world, as complete and unshakeable as her father's faith in 'Providence' and her mother's profound delight in the Royal Family. Automatically, on leaving the Secretarial College at Ipswich, Rosemary had taken over most of the counter work of the sub-office, typed business letters, checked invoices, and answered the telephone. Up to the age of twenty-three she was still perfectly happy with this arrangement: still a devoted and obedient daughter, she was engaged to be married, eventually, to Jack Butcher, a local farmer's son.

But suddenly and alarmingly her complacency was shaken one evening, by the announcement on the radio that a ship had been torpedoed in mid-Atlantic. No less than three hundred and twenty British children had miraculously escaped death, en route to friends and relations in Canada. Three of the children had been pupils in her own Sunday School class.

This one incident, with its appalling significance, had seized upon her sleeping imagination, and awakened a new compelling sense of urgency. What was she doing here, at her age, in the safe environment of a reserved occupation?

'London? You're joking, surely?' She could still see her Father's stricken face, hear the sharp annoyance in her Mother's voice, 'Don't be absurd, dear, we can't possibly manage without you.'

But they *had* managed with a young girl of sixteen and an old man of seventy, though it had taken a whole week to convince them she was serious and determined. Nobody was indispensable.

In a Lombard Street Bank she had taken over the duties of a young male clerk who had recently been recruited into the formidable ranks of the Fleet Air Arm. Three evenings, and one night a week she served as a reserve ambulance driver with the A. Division of St John's.

Christine and Gail, in the adjoining room on the top floor of the apartment house, had been friendly and sociable. Rosemary had no life of her own, and they insisted on sharing everything with her, even their boy friends! They lived in a frantic whirl of love affairs and 'dates' with American servicemen, and both were determined to add their names to the long list of GI brides, ready for exportation to the States.

From her sheltered little world, in a Suffolk village, Rosemary was dropped abruptly into the whirlpool of war-time London. Her one consuming dread, of losing her nerve on ambulance duty, was hidden under a false gaiety, to match the recklessness of her companions. But beneath this cloak of gaiety, she was lonely and desperately afraid, till she met Tony, with his quiet confidence. She knew only that he was completely honest and trustworthy, that she enjoyed his company, and waited for his shy fleeting smile as one awaits the rare glimpse of the rainbow, She also knew that he was very much in love with his wife, Joan, and adored his two young children.

Then, why did she not avoid him, instead of making every opportunity for meeting, by travelling on the same train, or waiting at the street corner near his lodgings? She could not help herself for she was in love and she had no pride left. When they met and exchanged a smile and a handclasp, she knew her eagerness and vulnerability was evident in her eyes, and the trembling of her whole body.

But the weeks went by, and still they had never once been alone together—completely alone. And Tony had not kissed her. She sometimes wept a little, on the way back to the square. Would they never be alone? Was it too much to ask?

'We can still be friends, can't we, Tony?' she had pleaded, one evening, when he seemed reluctant to make definite plans for the following Sunday.

Then he had smiled, and capitulated. Her heart had melted with strange new emotions, unlike anything she had ever known with Jack Butcher. As his eyes flickered over her face, she felt the hot flush flooding her cheeks and was ashamed of her own audacity—her own deliberate mishandling of a situation that should have been closed.

But Tony was reluctant only because his feelings for Rosemary were getting out of hand. His was not a sensual nature and he recognised the symptoms of sensuality in Rosemary's immaturity. To indulge in casual sexual intercourse for the temporary gratification of the senses was repugnant to his acute fastidiousness. But this was different. He could so easily love this girl, he reflected. Her glowing health was a stimulus to his frailty, her vitality attracted him. And she was so incredibly naïve! He could read her like a book, and observe all her little pretences. Her eyes held a childlike candour in keeping with her plump cheeks and flaxen hair. She had beautiful teeth, he noticed, and he liked to watch her bite greedily into an apple. Her healthy country appetite was appeased by slices of home-made cake and pies she brought back after her regular, monthly visits to Suffolk. But his own appetite was poor, and his landlady not at all clever at disguising whale steaks, powdered egg, and the inevitable Spam.

The asthma attacks had increased since he met Rosemary, and he carried a small inhaler in his pocket, but she was not yet aware of this. So when he smiled and capitulated, that evening, it was because he was too tired to argue, and it was easier to agree than refuse—

'Okay—same time, same place, if I don't see you during the week,' he told her.

Then came the Sunday when it was too wet and windy for their usual rendezvous, and Rosemary had phoned his lodgings to invite him round to her place for tea. Waiting for a bus, in a biting wind, Tony shivered, and started to cough. He wished he hadn't promised so readily. An afternoon in the easy chair, with one of Agatha Christie's mysteries, would have suited him better, he decided, miserably.

But when he stood in the doorway of her little bed sitting-room—gasping for breath after climbing the stairs—her warm, welcoming smile was very comforting. Closing the door softly, he sighed with resignation, and settled into the chair beside the gas fire, while she filled the little brown tea-pot, and tucked it into a hand-knitted cosy.

Feasting his eyes on her glowing cheeks and sturdy body, he knew it was impossible to deny her what she wanted, and that he had to sleep with her to find any relief from his own tormented mind. Mentally and physically, he was slipping into a state of degeneration. Too tired to go on alone, he missed Joan and the children intolerably. It was going to be a long war.

He could feel an attack coming on, and there was no escape. Those invisible hands he had grown to dread, were squeezing the breath from his lungs and tightening his throat. Great drops of sweat gathered on his brow. His eyes were dark and frightened.

'Tony!'

Rosemary's face puckered as she pushed the tea table aside and stood over him. Feebly he gestured towards the coat on the door, and she understood what he wanted and found the inhaler. Holding it firmly over his quivering face, he was conscious only of her nearness and strength; of her rounded breasts, under the tight hand-knitted jumper. Her swimming eyes held his frightened ones with consistent tenderness, and he seemed to drown in their liquid depths, in a great sorrow that he hadn't been able to spare her, after all. She knelt on the floor at his feet; her mouth tremulous, her cheeks wet with her tears, while he clutched her free hand convulsively. It was cold, and she was very frightened.

Gradually his chest expanded, and he breathed deeply of the Asthmosana. His eyes widened with relief. Then he pushed the inhaler away, and grinned boyishly, while Rosemary sponged his face.

'Oh, Tony—darling!'

Her arms went round him. He buried his head in her breast, and lay there exhausted, but happy, listening to the thud of her racing heart.

Some time later, he stretched luxuriously, took her face between his hands and kissed her gently. She fastened her arms about his neck, and her warm, wet mouth clung passionately to his thin grey lips. He felt her trembling body pressing closer, and all her yearning. Then he smiled his shy, indulgent smile, pushed her away, and stood up, staggering slightly, to turn the key in the lock. Her gay little curtains shut out the wintry sky, and the bare branches of the trees in the square. In the warm glow of the gas fire she was pulling the tight woollen jumper over her head, and her skirt lay on the floor. As in a dream, he walked across to her, and began to take the pins from her hair, marvelling at the shape and strength of her rounded shoulders, and the fullness of her breasts. There was no immaturity here! He was nothing more than a shadow and she the substance of love. Yet they needed each other so desperately now.

* * * * *

The Professor had a regular 'date' now in Piccadilly, with two GIs, called Hank and Joe. He had met them quite by chance, one wet afternoon, when his sensitive nostrils caught a whiff of fragrant coffee, as the doors of a milk bar swung open.

'Rainbow Corner', he read over the entrance, and then he remembered it was a rendezvous for all the young Americans swarming into London from the provinces. It was a gay, friendly place, with a juke-box pouring out a non-stop selection of dance tunes and sentimental songs. Behind the counters several pretty girls were serving refreshments to the row of customers on the red stools.

'Hiyyah! Santa Claus! Looking for someone?'

Two laughing boyish faces had swung round from the counter.

'The coffee,' he faltered 'it smells so good—am I permitted, or is it only for servicemen?'

'Sure you're permitted, come right in, Sir!' grinned the thin lanky boy, with a freckled nose. 'Shall we introduce ourselves? I'm Hank, and this is Joe, he's my buddy,' and they pumped the Professor's hand exuberantly.

Joe looked slightly abashed.

'Professor? I'm sorry, Sir, I mean, for calling you Santa Claus.'

'But it was a compliment and I like it,' the old gentleman assured him.

Hank took his umbrella, and they helped him to a stool. He sat there dangling his legs, with the two young servicemen on either side, looking him over with interest and amusement.

They were clean, healthy, young men, he thought, in their neat, tailored uniforms. Their heads were cropped, and they both had gleaming white teeth. His eyes moistened as he glanced from one to the other, for he was always grateful for a friendly word, and a little kindness in his adopted country.

'Cawfie and doughnuts, for three, and make it snappy, Honey!' drawled Hank, to the pert little blonde behind the counter.

She tossed her head and demanded,

'What's the hurry, big boy? You Yanks is all the same, always in a blinkin' hurry. Beats me where you get all your energy. What do they feed you on besides hamburgers and doughnuts?'

'Steaks!' said Hank promptly.

When she came back five minutes later, Joe leaned over to whisper confidentially,

'Say, Honey, the Professor says he ain't never tasted a doughnut. Can you believe that?'

Hank was gaping incredulously.

'Where does he come from then?' asked the blonde.

'Prague.'

'Prague? Where's Prague?'

'Czechoslovakia.'

'Oh yea.'

The blonde raised her eyebrows, and gave the old gentleman another pitying glance. These foreigners were all alike, she thought, and she had no time for them. Why they couldn't even speak English!

Hank bit hungrily into his third doughnut, and ordered more coffee, as soon as their cups were empty.

After such a long period of strict rationing, the Professor was astonished to see such abundance. Some of the young men were actually eating *two* fried eggs and *two* hamburgers!

'Coffee and doughnuts—they go together like English bubble and squeak? he suggested mildly.

The boys looked puzzled.

'Say, what's bubble and squeak?' they asked, simultaneously.

'Cabbage and potato from Sunday dinner, in a fry-up on Monday.'

The boys shuddered.

'*Fried cabbage*?' choked Hank, in disgust, biting into his sixth doughnut. 'What sort of food is that, Professor? There ain't no vitamins in it, not A, B, C, or D. They sure do need some understanding, these folks, I just can't figure it out. Gallons of tea, fish and chips, and this bubble and squeak racket. But you got to hand it to 'em, Professor, they got guts! Yes, Sir! The Limeys can take it.'

'I *still* can't figure it out,' sighed Joe, pulling a little book from his pocket, 'But we got it all down. Take a look at this.'

"What To Do and What Not To Do in Britain—A Short Guide for Overseas Servicemen."

The professor read the title carefully, and scanned the pages. It was his turn to look puzzled.

'It is useless. The person who compiled this has obviously met only one class of society. Theory! What is theory, in human relationships? But of course you find it difficult to fraternise when you have too much of everything, and the British so little. They think you are—how do you say it—big-headed. I also thought you were big-headed. But today I have changed my mind of the whole American nation, because two American boys have shown me where I was wrong!'

'Let's go some place else?' Hank suggested.

When the Professor found himself in the Windmill Theatre,

some time later, sitting between his young American friends, he was neither surprised nor shocked to be entertained by a bevy of beautiful naked girls. Perhaps he had reached an age when nothing seemed to surprise or shock, and he studied the nude figures in this living tableau without embarrassment.

Joe and Hank exchanged a cheeky wink over the venerable white head, and Winston Churchill's victory sign signalled OK! Stretching out their long legs luxuriously, they settled down to enjoy themselves.

After the show they hailed a 'cab', handed in their guest with such deference that the driver imagined him to be a VIP— then paid his fare to the square. Stepping back on the pavement, they both saluted smartly.

The Professor leaned back, wiping his eyes, quite overcome with emotion at their warm friendliness and generosity.

* * * * *

Katie O'Brien, on the way to the top floor one evening, stopped dead in the passage at the sound of muffled sobbing. She was no more capable of ignoring a creature in distress than checking her own tears, and a swift spasm of compassion gripped her heart.

"Tis that poor Miss Bennet, now, crying her eyes out,' she told the child. Tapping gently on the door of Number Two she called softly, in her honeyed Irish voice.

'Can I be doing anything for ye now? Will ye not open the door to me, Miss Bennet, m'dear?'

After a long moment, when she half expected to be rebuffed, the key was turned in the lock, and she crept in nervously, closing the door behind her. In the semi-darkness she saw her tenant glide across the room, and peer out of the window.

'The Colonel's cat—it's staring at me! It's still there, can you see it on the tiles?' she gulped, her body shaken with sobs.

Katie O'Brien stared out of the window, but saw nothing but the sloping roof, and a huddle of broken chimney pots. Then she looked at the face of the woman half hidden in the black-out curtain, and was shocked by the strange expression in the dark eyes. She had expected to see them flooded with tears, but they were dry and the sobbing seemed to come from deep down inside the poor creature and strangled in her throat.

One hand covered her mouth in a desperate attempt to stifle her cries. The child buried her face in her mother's shoulder, and clutched her tightly round the neck, and the warm little arms reminded her how lucky she was to have someone to cuddle and scold, someone to share her bed. Her eyes flooded with tears, and she seized the cold, trembling hand in a warm grasp.

'Don't be upsetting yourself now, m'dear, 'tis just fancy,' she sniffed. 'There's no cat there, at all, at all, for I saw it meself with me own eyes lying dead in the yard, so I did now! And I wrapped it up in an old towel, and the milkman took it away to bury it. That's the truth that I'm telling you, but I've not breathed a word to a living soul, till this very day.'

Miss Bennet still stared vacantly out of the window.

'It's still there, I can see it,' she said, decidedly.

But she allowed herself to be pushed gently into the chair, where she sat twisting her handerkchief into a tight ball. Her face looked pinched and grey, her mouth hung open, and loose strands of hair hung over her collar.

Katie O'Brien suddenly saw the perfect solution: a change is as good as a rest.

'There's David's room, next door, and it's still vacant. It's smaller than this one and not so light, but couldn't I be moving you in now this very day? If you could manage for the duration with David's single wardrobe, and the small chest-of-drawers, I could change the beds around, and the chairs, so it wouldn't be feeling so strange. Glory be! Isn't that the answer to the problem now, and no trouble at all, at all!'

Miss Bennet sighed, and her eyelids fluttered,

'Thank you, Mrs O'Brien. You are very kind,' she whispered, faintly.

Perhaps for the first time in two years she had seen the housekeeper as something more than a rather common little Irish woman, with slovenly habits. Or perhaps, on the verge of a nervous breakdown, she was so desperately in need of kindness and reassurance, anyone could have persuaded her, that evening. She sat there quietly, while Katie O'Brien hurried back to the basement, to make 'a nice strong cup of tea'.

*   *   *   *   *

I was listening to Vera Lynn, the Forces' Sweetheart,

singing her popular song hit—'We'll meet again, don't know where, don't know when'—when Katie tapped on my door.

'Of course I'll come and help you move the beds and the chairs around,' I told her, after I had listened to her story.

I had promised Mother to see the doctor. She insisted that I needed a tonic, an *iron* tonic because I was looking very 'peaky'. To please her, I finished work an hour early one evening and went along to the surgery in Queensway, and joined the patients in the crowded little waiting room. A chair was vacated within a few minutes, and I sat down beside a plump little woman with her hair in curling pins, and her feet in felt slippers, who introduced herself as Rosie, and seemed to know everyone. They were all 'regulars' she told me, and she looked me over with interest as a newcomer.

'Makes yer laugh, don't it ducks, this 'ere lark. Waste a time I calls it. Come back and see me next week, Rosie, 'e says, an' that's been going on for three weeks already. What's the matter with me then, Doc, besides me varicose veins, I says. Nervous exhaustion, Rosie, 'e says, or you can call it blitz fever, if you like. Everybody's getting it, stands to reason. Take it easy, Rosie, 'e says. Go 'ome an' put yer feet up! Then 'e gives me a certifikit, see. What's that for, Doc? I says, cheeky like. That's to put you off work, for a week or two, 'e says. Then I told 'im straight. But I only wants a tonic, Doc, then I'll be OK. You'll do as you're told for once in your life, my good woman, 'e says. Makes yer laugh, don't it?' chortled Rosie happily.

But the circle of weary, despondent faces did not seem to share her cheerful philosophy. They let her talk because it helped to pass the time, and there was nothing fresh to read. Several pre-war copies of the *Tatler* and *Country Life* had been discarded as being too highbrow. But there was no need for me to bother with magazines, with Rosie at my elbow.

'What jer think about this latest lark of 'itler's, ducks?' she demanded. 'Dropping bombs on all them lovely Cathedral cities. What does 'e expect to get out of it? I arsk yer? Took 'undreds of years to build them lovely cathedrals. It's a blinkin' shame. I got a married daughter living in Exeter with four kids, evacuated for the duration. They got a cathedral there, they tells me, but I got a letter from Glad only yesterday, and she said not to worry for they was alright so far. Makes yer laugh though, she telling me and 'er dad not to worry, when they're living in one of them so-called Safe Areas. You an' dad ought to come an' live with us, Mum, for the duration, says Glad, last year. Not me, Glad, I says, not your Dad neither. We ain't movin' out of Number Seventeen till we're blasted out!'

Another chortling laugh from the irrepressible Rosie roused only a mild titter of amusement from the other patients, but perhaps they had heard it all before. Then she turned to me.

'What's yer trouble, then? Look a bit washed out to me.'

'Nothing serious, I'm just here for a check up.'

'Well, don't forget to arsk for a certifikit. It's proof, see, that yer not pulling a fast one! So long, ducks! Good luck!'

It was Rosie's turn for the consulting room, and she gave me the thumbs up sign, as we passed in the doorway five minutes later.

But I didn't get a 'certifikit' for I was only suffering from a mild form of anaemia. But I *did* get an iron tonic, and a chit for an extra half pint of milk each day, so Mother would be satisfied!

*   *   *   *   *

I had a young nephew now, William's son. Surprisingly, the first child of the new generation was a replica of Father, with red curling hair, freckles and a most engaging grin, but without his grandfather's temper and temperament. He was a gentle, quiet child, who shied away from crowds and shops and noise, and seemed to inherit, from William, a passionate love of the country. William was serving as an Acting Major in a Kent Regiment, somewhere in Italy, and the boy was living in Worthing with his mother.

Living and working in London, I caught only a glimpse of my young nephew when I went home every fourth Sunday. My meagre salary at the Ministry, did not allow for private travelling, and since I had never been at all clever in budgeting my income, I often found myself walking to work, from Bayswater to Millbank, after spending a precious half-crown in a second-hand book shop! The walks were probably beneficial to my health, but wore out my shoes too quickly. The soles of the cheap 'utility' footwear must have been made of compressed cardboard, for they almost disintegrated in a heavy shower of rain, and were so thin at the ball of the foot, my shoes were invariably padded with newspaper.

Utility clothes were all of poor quality and poor workmanship. Coats, dresses, skirts and blouses had a uniform sameness that seemed to suggest they were turned out like sausages from some gigantic machine. Good, pre-war clothes could still be bought, at fantastic prices, for those who had money and coupons to spare. Clothing coupons had been regarded as a source of currency from the start, and in my world of small incomes, meagre rations and 'making do', we all sold coupons to more fortunate girls and women, whose husbands or boy friends provided the cash for new clothes. The average price paid, in my immediate circle, was two shillings per coupon, but we heard rumours of much higher rates in the Soho 'black market'. I was perfectly happy, however, to exchange five clothing coupons for ten shillings, and to know the momentary pleasure of having these extra shillings to spend on such luxuries as second-hand books, a visit to the cinema and a meal at a Lyons Corner House.

The Corner Houses, and all the Lyons tea-shops I frequented, provided me with plenty of light entertainment. The avid curiosity I had known since early childhood was nourished by the extraordinary variety of customers, their choice of food and their method of eating it! It varied from the delicate poising of the little finger over the teacup, to wiping the plate clean with a chunk of bread!

The customers, in war-time London, could well be called 'cosmopolitan', for they included displaced persons from all the European countries, Colonial volunteers, Indian and African students, and the biblical Tower of Babel could not have contained more strange tongues than a Lyons Corner House on a Sunday evening in the second year of World War Two! I found it fascinating and amusing, for I seldom sat for more than a few minutes at an empty table before being joined by some lonely or bored man of any age from seventeen to seventy.

'You have such a pleasant face,' I was told, or 'you look nice and homely.'

I received several invitations to renew the brief acquaintance the following Sunday, or to visit the 'flicks' or even to take a little stroll down Piccadilly. I refused them all, with a strange contradiction of eagerness and wariness—for I still hadn't completely recovered from the affair of the handsome ship's officer and its impact on my emotions. I was reluctant to get involved with another man, perhaps more than a little afraid of the consequences, especially in wartime, and I could not trust myself to a platonic friendship, much in favour at this period. Thus, a little shy of strange men with revealing eyes and beguiling voices, I stayed alone, and preserved my virginity! In a sense, the Ministry and the apartment house provided all I needed at this period, with a visit home once a month. Like most families separated by the war, the close bonds of our relationship seemed to weaken, as the nature of our individual lives and work became more demanding. I had no desire to linger for more than a day under the comparatively safe roof of home, but hurried back to London, where roofs collapsed and crumbled around us. This was not courage or foolishness, but a very real sense of belonging to London, at this particular period. Nerves were taut, and I wept easily at a word of rebuke or misunderstanding. But otherwise I was unaffected by the blitz.

The park provided both solace and silence in the early morning after the 'all clear' sirens had died away. The trees were still there, magnificently untouched by blast and bombs, and I looked on them every day with fresh joy and hope, as a symbol of ultimate victory. Despair and despondency had no place in my thoughts, or my heart, while the trees remained standing. One evening I found a letter with an Irish postmark on the mantelpiece. I had sold my first short story and a cheque was enclosed for three guineas.

*　　*　　*　　*　　*

'Westminster Abbey, Houses of Parliament and the British Museum caught a packet last night. They've got a bloody nerve those bastards!' the postman announced indignantly, as he handed over the morning delivery of mail.

'Glory be! 'Tis sacrilege now!' breathed Katie O'Brien, more shocked by this single item of news than any she had heard of recent months, from her three main sources of information—the postman, the milkman and the dustman. She had all but forgotten the previous occasion of national outcry, when enemy action had demolished a wing of Buckingham

Palace, and prayers of thanksgiving had been offered in all churches, for the safe deliverance of Their Majesties.

Katie was much too excited now to concentrate on sweeping the stairs, and after the postman's early delivery of letters and news, left the front door open to listen for the dustman.

Old Joe Collins was a veritable mine of information, and it was never necessary to buy a newspaper on the days Joe emptied the dustbins. As soon as she heard the lids crashing in the backyard, Katie tucked the child under her arm, hurried down the passage, and called a greeting from her front doorstep,

'Morning, ducks,' said Joe amiably, leaning on a heavy bin. 'What jer got in 'ere, then? Feels like old Goering!'

Mrs O'Brien giggled, then her face resumed the solemn expression suited to the occasion.

'Shocking news today, Mr Collins, so it is now. The cheeky monkeys to be dropping their bombs on Westminster Abbey and the Houses of Parliament!'

'And the British Museum,' Joe reminded her, for he knew she had already met the postman and the milkman, both equally garrulous with vital statistics, and inclined to exaggerate the damage, or enlarge on the horrors they had witnessed on their respective rounds. Nevertheless, he still had a trump card up his sleeve! Lifting his greasy cap to scratch his head, and planting one foot on the bottom step, he told her importantly.

'You ain't 'eard nothink yet, duck,' and paused dramatically, 'Rudolf 'Ess 'as landed 'isself in Scotland, straight out of the sky, as you might say, in one of them new parachutes.'

Mrs O'Brien looked puzzled, and her mouth drooped with disappointment.

'Never 'eard of 'im,' she declared, candidly.

'Never 'eard of Rudolph 'Ess? Cor!'

Joe wiped his sleeve across his sweating face, and coughed the dust from his lungs. 'Thought everyone knew about old 'Ess,' he ruminated. 'Calls 'isself 'itler's Deputy. Makes yer think, though, don't it? I mean ter say, somethink's gorn wrong over there in Germany, stands ter reason, 'itler's goin' to be blinkin' well mad over this lark. Put a real spanner in the works, this will. Running away from 'is beloved Fooyer, that's what 'es done alright, my ducks. Blinking well 'opped it out of Germany. Cor! I shouldn't 'arf like to see old 'itler's face when e 'ears all about it on the wireless!'

Joe smacked the seat of his corduroy trousers with malicious enjoyment. Mrs O'Brien, still suffering from her personal disappointment, sighed heavily, and suggested.'

"Ow about the other two—Goering and Goebbels? It's a fine chance to be making one or the other Hitler's Deputy.'

She liked Joe, but she wouldn't give him a second opportunity to catch her out, even if the name of Rudolph Hess had escaped her for the moment.

'Oh, but they got their own jobs to do, them two fellows, and they got their work cut out in their own departments,' argued Joe, warming to the topic of Hitler's Deputy. 'Old Goering's got the Loofworf to manage, more or less single-handed—that's German for the RAF,' he explained, 'and Goebbels is the 'ead of the Gestapo—that's the Secret Police over there. No, 'arf a mo', I got that wrong, old ducks, it's *'immler*, what's the 'ead of the Gestapo, not Goebbels. Yes, that's right, *'immler*.'

Mrs O'Brien agreed, for she was not going to admit she hadn't heard of that one either!

'Well, they all got ter 'ave another good 'ole 'anky-panky, after this 'ole lark today. Stands to reason, when one of the nobs does a bunk to Scotland without even a by-yer-leave from the boss, it's pretty serious, I can tell yer that much. Deserting the Fooyer and joining the enemy is what yer might call treason. They won't 'arf give 'im what for, if they catches up with 'im, the poor blighter. Still, they all got it coming to 'em, sooner or later. They can't win. Stands to reason, they got no blinkin' guts!'

And Joe heaved the heavy dustbin on to his shoulders, and staggered up the area steps. 'Bye-bye, ducks,' he called, leaving a trail of cabbage stalks in his wake.

*   *   *   *   *

I had been as surprised as Mrs O'Brien to discover Rosemary was pregnant, though not at all shocked by the discovery. Living apart from the family for so long, and embracing a wider, more tolerant world, my values had changed.

Mother was so steadfast and resolute in her values and principles she could accept no other valuation than the right and the wrong. Her mind was closed to prevarication, and her strong determination to see only these two alternatives—the right and the wrong—was so instilled in her children, I was compelled to feel guilty whenever I found a cause or excuse for straying into the channels beyond and between good and evil. William, Henry and Mary had all inherited Mother's admirable qualities of consistency and conservatism. With my own imperfections, I did not seek for perfection in others—only for truth and honesty, courage and humour.

Yet Mother's influence had been so strong, I was afraid this sense of guilt would persist throughout my life, whenever my thoughts, my intuition, or my will, clashed with hers. I could be swayed, convinced or persuaded to turn aside, to take another road, to change my mind or my opinions. This, to Mother, was weakness, and she could not tolerate such a condition in one of her children. Yet, I remembered her courage and fortitude, and still clung to the essence of her training and example.

'But Rosemary is such a *nice* girl, you would like her,' I insisted.

'Nice girls don't associate with married men!' was her final word on the matter, and she closed her lips firmly. She was very annoyed with me for condoning it. There was no excuse for trespassing on the sanctity of marriage, she had insisted, yet her own marriage was doomed from the start. How could such a marriage, in all honesty, be called sanctified? I had not dared to question Mother, even in my adult life, on what appeared to be the only mistake she ever made—to marry Father. She would be furious.

My nerves, at this period of the war, were taut as the strings of a fiddle, and I went to the station feeling choked with remorse that I had left her annoyed or worried about the bad influence of my contemporaries, and the sordidness of the apartment house. Yet I had to see her once a month, to be reassured that at least one person was still sane, still completely unmoved by the chaos and clamour of war. But we hurt each other, and I was aware of the hurt in my inmost heart, as I had been aware of the misery in Rosemary's crumpled body on my bed, that evening she told me about Tony.

'It's all over, Mrs O'Brien knows,' she had sobbed, convulsively. When she lifted her face it was distorted and ugly, her eyes black with despair. Could this be the same glowing girl I had met on the stairs, only a week ago?

'What did Mrs O'Brien say?' I prompted, tentatively.

'She said Tony's landlady had phoned to give me a message. He had another bad attack of asthma Easter Sunday morning, and had been taken by ambulance to a hospital in Berkshire. He was not expected back at his lodgings.' Then she gulped, and added piteably, 'They have sent for his wife. He doesn't need me any more.'

I sat on the bed and rocked her in my arms. She was a big, strong girl, nearly twice my size, but I felt extraordinarily big and responsible that evening. I had heard Rosemary's dragging feet on the stairs, and her stifled sobbing as she crept past my door. Such desolation was better shared, I thought, and brought her in. I had taken a chance in supposing her to be one of those women who like a shoulder to cry on, and not the kind who creep away and hide their grief.

So it was all over? Well, I could understand and sympathise, for I had been through the same bitter experience of unrequited love. Perhaps we had both been too trusting, too inexperienced, too immature to be taken seriously? I sighed, in retrospect, as I hugged her shaking shoulders, and tucked a loose strand of hair behind her ear. What a nice, clean, wholesome creature she seemed to me then, and not at all like Mother's conception of the 'fallen woman'. Fallen from what? A pedestal?

'But he did love me, Sarah, I *know* he did,' she repeated.

'Of course he did, it was obvious,' I assured her. 'But he was married, dear, so his wife, naturally, has priority when her husband is as sick as Tony.'

'Yes, I suppose so,' she sighed, and twisted a wet handkerchief into a knot. 'I wish I knew the address of the hospital, then I could write to him. Nobody could object to a letter, could they?'

'You could ring his landlady,' I suggested.

Her face quivered with new hope, as she glanced at her watch.

'It's too late now, but I'll ring in the morning,' she smiled tremulously, and put up her arms to embrace me, on a sudden wave of gratitude for such an obvious suggestion.

'You'll be all right now?' She nodded vigorously, so I left her.

'You fool!' I scolded myself severely. 'What good will it do? The poor girl is only prolonging her torment. What is over and finished can never be restored. You should know!'

I looked down on the quiet square, and wondered why we cling so persistently to the tiniest shred of hope, when there is none?

Rosemary wrote her letter, but no reply came. For more than a month she watched the early morning postman round the square, and ran downstairs to be the first to snatch the letters from the mat. Every night she hurried back to search the letter rack in the hall passage. Hope faded, at last, and she dropped the heavy burden of profound disappointment, and went home for the week-end.

I saw more of her now, and she gradually slid away from the company of Christine and Gail. She had never really fitted in to their noisy and rather frivolous little world, but did not like to upset them. In a way, I believe, they were relieved to shed her, and glad to see us together. Two of a kind, I expect they thought, for we were both country born and bred, fresh-complexioned and wore no make-up. We also washed our own hair, went to Church on Sunday, and enjoyed nothing more exciting, in our spare time, than a walk in the park, with the housekeeper's child in a push-cart!

*   *   *   *   *

A few weeks later, Katie O'Brien decided to have a tea party in her basement bed-sitting room to enliven the spirits of her tenants, who all seemed to be suffering from war nerves, in one way or another. They were coming and going at such irregular hours she couldn't seem to catch up with them, so she spent all Saturday evening laboriously copying out invitations, to push under the doors. She hesitated for some time over the Colonel and Miss Bennet, but thought they might feel offended to be left out. She needn't have worried for neither accepted her invitation to tea with the genuine excuse of 'going on duty'.

It was then that Katie O'Brien had another of her marvellous 'brain-waves' which she explained to me on Sunday morning with her usual exuberance.

'It would be a fine chance to make a collection from the tenants, so it would now, and we could buy a fine pram for the poor innocent little lamb.'

I must have looked rather blank, for she went on to explain.

'Rosemary's baby—have you forgotten now she has only a few months to go, and nothing ready but a cot, and ten matinee coats,' she sighed, for it was an added responsibility on her shoulders.

'No, I haven't forgotten,' I told her. 'Does the landlord know that Rosemary is expecting a baby?'

She threw up her hands.

'Mercy of God! I shall never breathe a word to him now. He would have me turn the poor girl out into the street, the miserable old sinner!'

'But how will you manage to hide the fact there's a baby in the house, and where will Rosemary keep the pram, if not in the passage?'

'In my scullery,' she told me promptly.

'How often does the landlord visit the place'?

'Once in a blue moon, m'dear, and there's no need to worry at all at all. He'll not be anywhere near London during the raids, for he's much too careful of himself.'

'Good, that seems to dispense with your biggest worry. Now, about that collection. You could hardly ask the Colonel and Miss Bennet to contribute towards a pram, for a start, and the Zolameks have very little money, surely, as refugees? I don't know about the Professor, he seems a decent old boy, but Mrs P might refuse, and that only leaves you and me! Anyway Rosemary's not going to like it.'

She looked so disappointed I pointed out that we might raise enough money between us to buy a second-hand 'tansad', from the shop in Westbourne Grove, but a new pram was much too expensive.

Then I helped to cut the Spam sandwiches, and she went off to the pastry shop with the child to buy a sickly looking 'gateau' oozing with synthetic cream. I borrowed cups from the girls, and the Professor generously offered half his sugar ration for the week. The big enamel teapot with the chipped spout, which Mrs O'Brien had bought in the junk shop for ninepence, would probably take most of her tea ration, but she wasn't worried, for she would beg, borrow or steal, later in the week, if necessary.

The child was wearing a new siren suit, modelled on the lines of Mr Winston Churchill's, and she refused to be parted from it. She even went to bed in it, her mother told me. She was growing into a pale, puny little girl, owing to her mother's erratic feeding. She ate what she liked, had no regular meal-times, and seemed to survive on a diet of sausages and chips, cakes and strong tea.

'Don't be taking any notice of the child, now, for she's come over shy,' Katie O'Brien explained to her guests, as they assembled in the basement. So we left her alone, sitting under the table with a cake in each hand to keep her quiet.

Papa and Mama Zolamek, who had some difficulty getting down the basement stairs, and could not understand why they were asked to take tea in the housekeeper's room, sat perched on the edge of her bed, looking extremely uncomfortable.

The Professor, who had been given the only comfortable chair, leapt to his feet as soon as Mrs P arrived, but his gallantry was rather wasted for she insisted on fetching a chair from the scullery, and sat on the edge, with a rather sulky expression on her face. Perhaps she was tired and her Sunday afternoon rest had been disturbed, and she might also have been wondering if the tea party was just an excuse to announce an increase in the rent.

I sat on the window-sill, looking out on the yard, with its over-flowing dustbins, and rubble. The marmalade cat lay stretched on the roof of the coal-shed, playing with a dead sparrow. I thought of Mia, and wondered if the Colonel was still searching for her.

Then Katie O'Brien, flushed and excited, rushed in with the teapot, exclaiming breathlessly,

'Sure and it's grand to see you all—so it is now!'

When all her guests were served with tea and I had handed round the sandwiches, she sat down on the fender, gathered the child on her lap, and explained about the pram, and the 'collection', with such an air of mystery concerning the baby it must have been extremely puzzling to the Professor and Mrs P. Then came an awkward pause, when I grabbed a plate, dropped my own contribution of five shillings in, and handed it round rather self-consciously. Mrs P anxiously searched her purse for a shilling, but looked at me suspiciously. The Professor added a half-crown, and the Zolameks, who hadn't understood a word of Katie O'Brien's story, seemed to think they had to pay for their tea, and Papa put a florin in the plate, with a puzzled frown. Katie O'Brien was delighted with the response and added a grubby ten shilling note to the collection.

This puzzled her guests even more. Why should the house-keeper give ten shillings to her own fund? And who was expecting a baby? Mrs P and the Professor exchanged a glance of mild surprise, then shrugged their shoulders.

'Plis, vee may go?' asked Papa Zolamek politely, when all was apparently settled to everyone's satisfaction. Mystifying people the British. 'It vas a pleasure,' he told the housekeeper, with a stiff little bow and helped Mama off the bed.

As they slowly climbed the stairs, she was clearing her throat, and rolling her tongue around her mouth.

'It is the tea, Mama. It leaves a bad taste in the mouth. I make coffee, h'ugh? Nice strong, black coffee!'

He kissed her pallid cheek, took her hand, and led her carefully back to their own apartment, with the patience born of their mutual suffering and isolation. Some nights he was tormented by a dream, in which they wandered, hand in hand, through the streets of a strange city, searching, always searching for their lost children.

*　　*　　*　　*　　*

Nothing had been said between us about Mrs O'Brien's tea-party, and the collection for the pram, but when I discovered Rosemary varnishing the wheel spokes of the 'tan-sad' pram, in the backyard, one Saturday afternoon, I went down the area steps to speak to her about it.

'I'm sorry about that collection,' I began, tentatively. 'But it was Mrs O'Brien's idea, entirely, and she had been so decent about everything, it seemed a pity to discourage her.'

Her candid eyes met mine unflinchingly,

'I have never been so embarrassed in my life,' she confessed. 'I was saving for the pram, anyway, and she needn't panic. The baby is not due till November.'

'I know, and it must be so annoying to have everyone trying to run your life for you, and buying things you would rather choose for yourself. I'm afraid I've been guilty of too much impulsive buying, myself, but I managed to wangle a few more clothing coupons from one of the girls in the office.'

'That's all right, I don't mind you, that's different,' she sighed, and straightened her aching back, while I admired her handiwork. 'I like these messy sort of jobs, but I'm not much good at knitting, and I seem to be sitting back comfortably while other people do it. Everyone is spoiling me dreadfully, and I really am terribly grateful, Sarah, though I do get a bit huffed at times. Take no notice, expectant mums are allowed a bit of temperament, so I'm told! Let's sit down, I feel about ninety—it's just one of those days.'

She spread the pram cover on the area steps, and we sat down companionably, side by side.

'Just look at the size of me—must be twins!' she chuckled. Then suddenly her face was still and pensive. 'I felt my baby move for the first time, last night. It was the most wonderful thing that has ever happened to me,' she said, and clasped my hand. 'Now I know it lives and breathes and has its own separate identity, I can wait. It's a funny thing, but I've almost forgotten Tony, in the past few weeks. Would you believe it, when I was so passionately in love with him? Now I know I am all maternal, and would make a very unsatisfactory wife anyway.'

I squeezed her shoulders affectionately.

'What nonsense you talk! You will make some lucky man very happy one day.'

She shook her head.

'I have met only two kinds of women—good wives and good mothers. A woman who combines both qualities is very rare, in my opinion. It would seem that a woman either spoils her children and neglects her husband, or neglects her children and spoils her husband!'

'You could be right. We once had a neighbour who said the same thing.'

'I'm not very maternal, at the moment, but perhaps I should feel like you, if ever I have a child.'

'Perhaps—though I think maternity is there, from the beginning. Look at most small girls with their dolls. Were you a lover of dolls?'

'No—books, always books!'

'Well, of course, you *could* be one of the brilliant exceptions to the rule, but no, I think I can see you as a doting wife, with a husband who adores you!' she reassured me gaily, then her thoughts swung back to the child in her womb. 'It completely absorbs me now, Sarah, I don't even think about the war, honestly, I feel nothing but joy and contentment, and a lovely sort of satisfaction in my strong healthy body, because my baby will be strong and healthy too. It's strange though, that I see no future for us, and make no plans. I suppose I should?' she smiled, and dropped her head on my shoulder. 'Just look at that cat! It's stalking that poor little sparrow. I hate that ginger cat, it's got an evil face,' she shuddered. 'I wonder if the poor old Colonel is still pining for his precious Mia? I believe that queer Miss Bennet had something to do with it. It was odd that she had a nervous breakdown about that time'.

'And Mrs O'Brien was marvellous,' I reminded her, 'Miss Bennet would probably have been sent away for treatment, if Katie hadn't taken care of her.'

'Dear Katie! By the way, have you ever seen her husband?'
'No.'

'It's a queer sort of household, Sarah, we know so little about each other, yet all living under the same roof. You would think the war would have brought us closer together, and those horrible nights of the blitz—but it hasn't, and we are still comparative strangers. I like dear old Papa Zolamek, though. He's such a poppet. Do you know, he actually stopped me in the square this morning to offer his congratulations! He must have been very puzzled that day at the tea party, but now it's so obvious he can't be mistaken!'

'I like the Professor. He's a real old aristocrat. Have you seen the courteous little bow he bestows on Katie when he meets her on the stairs? She would lick his boots, she's so pleased!'

At that moment the scullery door opened and the child came out to join us. We made room for her on the step, and she sat between us, with her small hands folded in her lap.

'I'll be putting on the kettle, m'dears, now. I've finished with the cleaning for another week,' her mother called out cheerily. 'Sure, there's never a dull moment these days, m' darlins, 'an likely as not we shan't be handing in our notice after all!'

We looked at each other over the child's head, and smiled. We were all Katie's children now.

*   *   *   *   *

'There is a baby in the house,' Mama Zolamek pronounced, 'I can *smell* the baby,' she added definitely.

Papa Zolamek, astounded by her eloquence—it was the longest speech she had made in two years—stood spellbound on the doormat holding their blankets and bundles. They were still sleeping in the Underground, and their daily routine had changed very little, while changes were taking place all around them, all the time. Katie O'Brien kept them informed of all that was happening under the communal roof, but since they understood only about one word in ten of her rich Irish brogue, their impressions were curiously mixed and muddled. Several of the faces they had seen in the early days at the apartment house had disappeared altogether.

They had liked the young man with the tousled hair and heavy features, and the nice, familiar name of David, and had always shaken hands with him whenever they met, indoors or out. Papa would ask anxiously, 'You are vel, David, yes?' David always answered the same way, 'Yes, thanks, I'm okay.' A nice boy, and so clever with the music like their own little son, Benjamin. But there the resemblance ended, for Benjamin had been a handsome, dark-eyed boy, olive-skinned, slender as a wand, with a shapely head, crowned with a wealth of gleaming black hair. There was the day that David came to see them, in a smart new uniform, and a new hair-cut. They had given him ten shillings, because they understood from Katie O'Brien that he was always short of money, But Papa was afraid he had made a mistake, for the poor young man looked so embarrassed. He was always making mistakes in the country of his adoption, and would never get used to its extraordinary contradictions. The language was still a barrier, separating them from the friendly and familiar faces of their restricted environment. But after the episode of the ten shillings, and everyone on the doorstep to watch David step into a taxi, he had driven away, and not returned. That was some time ago.

Papa had also wondered why they were asked to contribute money at Mrs O'Brien's tea party. Then he had discovered it was the girl, Rosemary, who was having the baby. It was all very confusing.

Looking at their faces now, so seamed with suffering, you would suppose they were the grandparents, not the parents of those three, lovely, lively children, thought Papa Zolamek, sadly. They would never be young again. Middle-age had passed them by altogether, and now they were old, in appearance, and in their slow, clumsy movements. But the hardest part of all to bear had been Mama's deadly apathy. She was alive, yet not living—a body without a spirit. His patience was inexhaustible, and his loving compassion excused and protected her from all the strange and bewildered confusion and commotion surrounding them since they first arrived in London. Now, at last, a glimmer of hope and encouragement for his long endurance.

It was so sudden, so surprising, Papa could do nothing but stand on the doormat, tears oozing from behind his steel-rimmed spectacles, while Mama, more than a little exasperated by his slow response, repeated, clearly and decisively,

'There is a baby in the house. I can *smell* the baby.'

'Yes, Mama, you are right.'

His face puckered with relief and joy, as he peered at her closely, waiting for further enlightenment. It had been unnatural and completely foreign to his nature to assume leadership and responsibility, but the past few years had shown him no alternative. Her eyes were still dry, he noticed, and devoid of all expression. She had shed no tears since that terrible day the children disappeared. Her heart had died that day. She was empty and drained of the spirit that had sustained her—until today.

Now she stood, transfixed, sniffing the scent of a baby, as any female animal sniffs the scent of her young. To Papa Zolamek, however, the smells of the apartment house were the same today, yesterday and always—the damp smell of raincoats in the passage, the greasy smell of fried sausages and chips drifting up from the basement, the faint scent of eau-de-cologne, when the genteel Miss Bennet passed by, the pleasant whiff of the Professor's pipe, the clinical smell of Wright's Coal Tar soap, in the bathroom, after Mrs P had washed her hair—and the nicest smell of all, the aroma of their own coffee.

'You have no nose for this smell of baby, never!' Mama scolded, with some asperity, as they started up the stairs. On the landing she stopped to sniff again. 'Here it smells only of that horrid, yellow soap. The baby, it is downstairs,' she said.

Papa, as always, loaded like a pack mule, dropped everything to the floor, and unlocked the door of their apartment. But today he hadn't to lead Mama by the hand to her favourite chair, and remove all her outside garments, for she strode past him, and paced the floor like a caged lioness, staring about her as though she were seeing it for the first time. Then, with a sudden gesture, both fierce and frightening, she threw up the window, and leaned out dangerously,

'Mama! No!'

Papa rushed to save her, with pleading, imploring hands. But she turned to look at him, and now he saw scorn in those dark eyes—eyes that for so long had been empty of all expression.

'You think I want to jump out of the window? Never! You should know me better than that.'

He felt a little foolish, but it was no new feeling—rather was it a faint echo of the past, and he welcomed it now, for he was so very tired. While he was a humble pastry cook she had been the only daughter of a bank official. Now the old regality seemed to be flowing back into her sagging body, as he stood there, watching her with a pathetic sort of wonder and admiration. Her back straightened perceptibly, and her shoulders squared. Then suddenly she was conscious of her loose, untidy hair, and both hands swept the heavy coil from her neck and restored it firmly to the crown of her head, where she pinned it securely. She looked much younger now, but her face was stony, and her mouth set obstinately.

'Make the coffee!' she commanded, in a curiously taut voice, while she stood at the open window, breathing deeply of the fresh, damp air, as though starved of it for too long. Her matronly bosom heaved spasmodically under the tight black jumper that Miss Bennet had collected from the WVS clothing depot. They had both been dressed entirely from this depot, but Mama had shown no appreciation or gratitude for this service, but accepted it, as she had accepted everything, with the same indifference. Now she was inspecting the tight jumper and thick ungainly skirt, more closely, and wondering how she came to be wearing such ugly garments.

The familiar aroma of coffee drifted across to her, but for once in her life, it had no quality of refreshment. The long-remembered, delicious smell of babies was still in her nostrils. No other smell could compensate today. A door had been open at the end of the passage, one of the many doors she would now like to enter, for perhaps she could solve the mysteries of this house. Her mind had not been so blank as Papa had imagined, and she had retained quite a lot of the housekeeper's excited chatterings, though confused and muddled. Did the baby belong to Mia, Mrs O'Brien, or one of the girls on the top floor?

Her head ached abominably, but she hated all kinds of mystery and deception.

'Someone tapping on the door. See who is there,' she told Papa, sharply.

Mystery and deception.

She had just remembered her children. It was flooding back now, into her opened, receptive mind—all the horror and humiliation, the terror and torment of their disappearance.

'Oh my God!'

Her anguished cry was lost in Papa's excited exclamation as he opened the door. She turned her eyes slowly, the horror still in her eyes, to see a flushed young woman, with a baby in her arms, standing hesitatingly in the doorway.

'Mama! See who is here!' he cried. Then in his halting, careful English, he said to the girl, 'Mama say she smell baby. Mama was right, yes?'

'Ask her to come in,' said Mama Zolamek, in a strained voice, from the window.

Rosemary walked in shyly, and, looking past the squat figure of Papa Zolamek, saw the ravaged face of his wife. 'Something dreadful has happened here,' she thought. 'This is not the same woman I have seen coming in and out, with blank eyes, holding her husband's hand like a child.' But she was no longer shy and hesitant, for now she knew why she had been prompted to call in with the baby, on her first day home from the hospital.

Smiling at the woman in the window, she went across to her, holding out the fat little bundle in the white shawl. The language of words was still a barrier, but the language of motherhood knew no barriers. Mama Zolamek's ashen face contorted painfully, and she trembled so violently as she took the child in her arms that Rosemary caught her breath, fearful for its safety. The baby gazed up at the woman with blue, translucent eyes, and its round, cherubic face, swathed in the shawl, was the most beautiful thing she had seen for a very long time.

'Benjamin,' she whispered, brokenly. But Benjamin had been even more beautiful, with his raven-black hair, and eyes of velvet. This child had a Saxon fairness of skin and eyes, with only a smudge of hair, soft and downy as a small day-old chick. She feasted her eyes on this miracle of loveliness and light, from a world so dark she felt she could never find the way back. As she groped for a light in the sudden torment of realisation, this scrap of humanity had been dropped into her arms, warm and soft and sweet-smelling.

Then the tears came slowly and painfully, hot and heavy with their long pent-up imprisonment. She could see them falling on the baby's head, and turned her face away quickly. Then she was laughing inexplicably, and she felt the laughter pouring from her throat as the tears poured down her cheeks. Laughing and crying, she asked the girl beside her,

'Vot you call 'im?

'John.'

'John.' She repeated the name and she liked the sound of it. It was easy to remember, not like so many of the English names they heard in the Underground. Papa was crying now—the silly man! Her laughter strangled in her throat while she scolded him, but even her scolding had an unaccustomed gentleness that surprised her.

'Why are you crying, Papa?' she asked.

He shook his head. Poor Papa! He was so overcome with emotion he couldn't begin to explain, and Mama's unpredictable behaviour was so disconcerting he was completely bewildered. Not only bewildered but anxious. What would happen now? Would she want to keep the baby? Would she make a dreadful scene when Rosemay took the child away?

He could see the girl was worried too, and her fears were probably the same as his own. But she accepted a cup of good, strong coffee, and sat down quietly, if a little nervously, to wait. They smiled weakly at each other over the coffee cups, but hardly dare take their eyes from the figure at the window. She was rocking the baby now, and crooning a rather sad little lullaby—wiping the tears away on the back of her hand. She seemed to be completely absorbed in her rocking and crooning, and her coffee grew cold in the cup. Quietly and patiently they waited, for they both knew the anguish she would suffer when that fat little bundle was removed. At last she spoke, very softly,

'John sleep,' she said, and sighed.

'Shall I . . take him . . now?' asked Rosemary.

Mama Zolamek handed over the fat little bundle, and asked pleadingly,

'You . . you kom back . . tomorrow, yes?'

'Yes, I will! I'll bring him every day to see you, Madame Zolamek, I promise! Every day,' she repeated, as she backed out of the room with her precious burden.

'Okay,' said Mama Zolamek, surprisingly.

*   *   *   *   *

Miss Bennet, who seemed to have taken on a new lease of life in David's old room, always asked to look at the baby as he was carried up and down stairs. In some extraordinary way, he seemed to have brought a new atmosphere of friendliness and sociability to the apartment house—a 'benediction' was Miss Bennet's word for it. This small infant we all adored had actually banished the ghost of Mia! No longer did those haunting blue eyes stare accusingly in the window, to remind her that once she had been a cruel and malicious woman. Obsessed by the ghost of Mia, her mind had become deranged for a time, and only Mrs O'Brien's kindness and common sense had saved her from being removed to a clinic for treatment. After a lifetime of repression, it was so difficult to show her *real* feelings and gratitude to the little Irish housekeeper. She knew it was most unladylike to be at all demonstrative, but one evening she allowed herself the luxury, and hurried downstairs with a fluttering heart. Mrs O'Brien called 'Come in!' from her basement bed sitting room, but Miss Bennet answered rather tremulously,

'It's only me! May I speak to you for a moment?'

As the door opened, the nice little speech she had prepared went clean out of her head and she blurted out, self-consciously,

'You must forgive me, Mrs O'Brien, for trespassing on your privacy, but I *had* to come—just to say—thank you! I couldn't wait a moment longer—I . . I . . ' Then she really lost control, burst into tears, and actually found her head on Mrs O'Brien's shoulder! They both cried—and then the child had cried, because she could never bear to be left out of anything! But now Miss Bennet was like a new woman, and had rejoined Mrs King on the WVS tea-trolley. 'It was really wonderful, the blessing of a new baby in the house,' she told Mrs King excitedly.

When John was a week old, and they were still both comfortably housed in the maternity wing of a big London hospital, evacuated to Oxfordshire, Rosemary sat down to write the most difficult letter of her life. After three attempts, she finally finished with a single page of note-paper, and a letter so brief, it seemed, in her tense and nervous condition, to be almost objectionable. Trying to soften the blow, she had only succeeded in stating the bald fact that she was a mother. She tried to imagine the shock and dismay on the faces of her parents, as they read the letter—and their reactions, when the initial shock was over. How would they react to this grave and totally unexpected crisis in their sheltered orderly lives? If only she could have spared *them* the shame and humiliation. She, herself, had no shame or humiliation—only a profound joy in motherhood, and a tremendous sense of fulfilment. But she knew, only too well, how cruel and spiteful the gossips could be, in a small community, especially when the guilty party had been a loved and respected member of that community, all her young life. She shivered apprehensively, as she sealed the letter for posting.

During the latter part of her pregnancy, she had postponed her monthly visits to Suffolk, until it was too late. But postponement had only added to the burden of her anxiety, and she still had to face them, eventually, with the truth, and with the child. Her letter was neither pleading nor penitent, yet, in her heart, she yearned for her home, and her parents' understanding. She was starting back on her job as soon as she got back to London, for she was getting desperately short of money.

'We can work out a sort of rota for looking after John when you are at work—if you like the idea?' I suggested, the day we welcomed them back to the apartment house.

Rosemary looked at me, and then at her son. Her glowing face and shining eyes were all the evidence I needed that she was still happy to be a mother and not in the least perturbed about the precarious future that faced them.

'Bless you all! What a lovely idea,' she said. 'By the way, are there any letters for me? I haven't seen any.'

Her bright eyes clouded for a moment, then she sat down carefully in my sagging little arm-chair, unbuttoned her cardigan, and put the baby to her breast so naturally, my throat tightened, with the poignant memory of another baby, and myself on a hassock, dimly aware of the warm intimacy between a mother and her child.

'I shall have to wean him when I start working—poor darling! I hope he won't be too upset,' she was saying.

It was then that she decided to call on the Zolameks, and I was amazed at the story she told me some time later. But why had Mama Zolamek recoiled from Mrs O'Brien's child, yet allowed the new baby to melt her frozen heart? That to me, was so unpredictable. Could it have been only the sense of smell—the one so sweet and the other so sour?

'She looked so strange, I was terrified she would drop John out of the window,' said Rosemary. 'But what could I do? I felt so helpless, I could only sit and wait.'

'Sitting and waiting was the most sensible thing to do, my dear,' I assured her. 'Poor soul, how dreadful the awakening must be. In a way, I suppose, she has been spared the mental torment a normal person would have endured these few years, but who can really say what the state of her mind has been like—a complete blank, or only partially numb?'

'My pity is all for Papa Zolamek, now that I have seen her amazing recovery. She will be simply unbearable to live with, and she talked to him with such condescension, as though he were beneath her,' said Rosemary. 'At least he knew he was the stronger character when he led her by the hand.'

'Perhaps he was not naturally the dominant partner, if Mama reverts back to this manner of addressing him?' I suggested. 'He seems to me to be rather a humble little man.'

'He's a poppet. For his sake I shall let her see as much of John as she wishes, but Katie expects top priority!'

'Katie *deserves* top priority!' I reminded her.

* * * * *

Before Rosemary left for work the following Monday morning, she carried her son downstairs, and tucked him in his pram in the yard. She had very definite ideas about fresh air.

'Fresh air!' wailed Katie O'Brien, 'in November? The poor little innocent will die of exposure, now!' And she wheeled him into the hot stuffiness of her basement bed sitting-room, as soon as his mother turned the corner of the square!

I knew this would happen, but I had no intention of telling

Rosemary what I had seen. A bit of extra coddling wouldn't harm a child, and he would get all the fresh air he needed in his mother's bedroom at night, for she always opened her window before she got into bed, whatever the weather. Well, he looked to have his mother's healthy robustness, for he was a big, strong infant, so he would probably thrive on these extremes of stuffiness and freshness!

Mama Zolamek, who had completely recovered her normal self, had flatly refused to spend any more nights in the Underground, and had everyone nicely organised for the 'rota' of baby-minding, during the day. She would collect him from Mrs O'Brien at ten o'clock, and keep him till twelve, so allowing the housekeeper two hours for her chores.

'I shall be plasing meself, now, when I do the cleaning, whether 'tis the morning or the afternoon!' said Katie indignantly. She couldn't bear to be 'organised', and came to the conclusion that she much preferred Mama Zolamek in her original state!

Miss Bennet, who had begged to 'take her turn', was asked to push him out for an hour in the afternoon, for an airing in the Park, for she agreed with his mother in the importance of Fresh Air!

Then the dear old Professor had offered his services, and would probably be allowed to mind both children in his room, while Mrs O'Brien popped out to do her shopping.

Christine and Gail had not been included on the 'rota', not because of their many engagements, but because they were considered too irresponsible.

The Colonel, whose interest in infants was negligible, was prompted to be a little more charitable and actually suggested the pram should be kept in his room, when not in use, as the scullery seemed hardly a suitable place.

'Glory be!' exclaimed Katie O'Brien, 'What's come over the man?'

Mrs P who was sorry for the grudging way she had contributed a shilling to the 'collection' that Sunday afternoon at Mrs O'Brien's tea party, was anxious to make amends, and saved up her tips at the hotel to buy a very large and very expensive teddy-bear.

'Everyone is so terribly kind. Even the girls at the Bank have given me presents for John, today,' Rosemary told me, the week before Christmas. Then she asked her usual question, 'Were there any letters for me today?'

I couldn't bear to see her disappointment day after day. What should I do if she had no letter from home before Christmas? Would Mother allow me to take Rosemary and the baby to share our Christmas? Whatever her objection to Rosemary she wouldn't be able to resist young John. Three days before Christmas the long-awaited reply arrived, in the shape of a telegram.

''Tis bad news now,' said Katie, who always trembled at the sight of the little orange-coloured envelopes.

I propped it on my mantelpiece, and awaited Rosemary impatiently. She usually arrived back about six o'clock, half-an-hour or so later than me, and I collected John from Katie and brought him upstairs ready for his bath and bottle. He was a friendly baby and seemed not to mind in the least that he was handled by everyone, and passed around all day like a little parcel. In fact he enjoyed all the spoiling and attention, but the arms of his mother were the arms he liked best.

She blew in, with a breathless eagerness, snatched him from my lap, and cuddled him close to her breast. Then her eyes darted to the mantelpiece, and the orange envelope, and her face paled.

'Shall I open it?' I asked, gently, for I had grown so fond of her, in the past six months, I should like to have spared her any more pain. Then I read the brief message, and passed it over to her, with a huge sigh of relief.

'Expecting you both for Christmas—All our Love—Mother and Dad.'

*   *   *   *   *

They travelled down to Suffolk on Christmas Eve, and I took them to Liverpool Street by taxi. It was the last I saw of them, for they never came back to London.

The deadly isolation of the top floor, after the Christmas holiday, was quite unbearable. Christine and Gail, both engaged to be married, were seldom seen these days, and when they did appear had no thoughts in their heads other than the wonderful plans they were making for a double wedding at Easter. Their anticipation of life in the States for a GI bride was as colourful and unrealistic as the films they had seen in the West End cinemas. I hoped, sincerely, they would not be too disappointed and disillusioned, for it seemed they knew hardly anything about their prospective in-laws, or their prospective homes, and even less about their prospective husbands! How could they bear to take such risks? It was quite beyond my comprehension. My risks were only with that vital part of me involved in exploration, curiosity and rebellion. (I could not foresee the day when I should risk everything— body and spirit, family and friends, reputation and religion, to the devastating attraction of one man.)

However, the girls' excitement only increased my isolation on the top floor, and I could not shake off the depression, or the gloom of that closed door across the landing. Once again I was tense with waiting for someone who would never return. Was it to be my destiny? Was it my own fault that I could not hold on to anyone? I was sorely troubled by this suggestion. An intangible bond held me bound to the family, that much I knew for certain—we *belonged*, together or apart. Perhaps my very independence was a barrier to lasting relationships? It was hard to define. Everyone blamed the war now for all the chaos and confusion in their lives. I heard myself saying to Christine and Gail, with a violence born of my loneliness and misery,

'I can't stand it! I shall find another job and move away from here! Nobody can stop me! There is nothing to keep me here now that I've lost Rosemary and John.'

Then I burst into tears, and ran downstairs—out of the front door, across the square, to Queensway, and over the busy Bayswater Road to the park—still running! But this was no new discovery—that I had to move on. Circumstances changed. Why blame the war? Why blame Rosemary for not coming back when she had promised? Should I come back in a similar situation? Of course not! 'Don't be ridiculous, and don't for heaven's sake, start feeling sorry for yourself. Self-pity is a soul-destroying state of mind,' I reminded myself, sternly, and shivered in the wind, without my overcoat. Reason was not my strong point, intuition was my driving force, but today I tried to reason, as I marched briskly down the long straight path between the trees.

It was Sunday afternoon again, too early for the regular

parade of people taking the air, for health's sake. The park was deserted but for a solitary man exercising his dog. The naked branches of the trees made extraordinary shapes and patterns against the grey sky—beautiful shapes and patterns, that held, for me, a sort of magic. Stripped of all their autumn glory, they had not died. They were sleeping.

My pulses stopped racing and my tears dried on my cheeks. Nothing was lost! It was only on the top floor of the apartment house I felt such emptiness and misery. It was the end of another chapter, not the end of everything. I always felt this way, as a chapter finished—a kind of death. But it would pass when I started to pack my things! This strange reluctance to close a chapter, already finished, was a contradiction of the eagerness with which I should start on the next! But now that I could laugh at myself again, I felt better.

Optimism was a state of mind I enjoyed most of the time, and depression seldom lasted long. In the tingling air my spirits soared, and overhead the barrage balloons swung lazily in the winter sky. The smell of wet earth and moulded leaves was sweet to my country-bred senses. The mournful cry of the gulls flying inland from the river was part of the winter day. The seasons came and went, unchanging in their pattern of regularity. Before the trees awakened from their winter sleep I should be out of London, I knew not where, but perhaps in the country? The thought refreshed me. I would never be a true Londoner, for such roots as I had were buried in the earth, not in concrete. I could spread my wings, yet still return to the earth, like a home-coming lark!

Thinking of beech woods, spread with a carpet of bluebells, sunshine and shadows on a furrowed field, yellow kingcups on the river bank, a white cloud of cherry blossom over the orchard and the hop vines hanging in long green arches, I reached Marble Arch. The grey-haired waitress in Lyon's tea-shop would lend me a shilling for a cup of tea and two slices of toast. We were very good friends since the time I had so many cups of tea at her table, in the company of young David, during the early days of the apartment house. Remembering David now, as I sipped my hot tea gratefully, I was reminded of the fun we had composing our songs. This also reminded me that I still had an invitation to write a short series of articles about children in other countries—the countries I had visited, before the war put a stop to my wandering.

I knew this creative urge had the power to comfort and compensate. It was something essentially mine, strong and resilient as the trees in the park. Although it was not a persistent urge—I could go for long periods without writing anything more than a few letters to family and friends—it was a part of me. The comforting reminder of pen and paper, together with a few quiet hours, had often restored my confidence and happiness, in the past. It was decisive thought and action, after so much muddled thinking and indecision, that I found so stimulating. I could not bear indecision. I had to know, to feel, to act. 'Make up your mind!' I would say, sometimes rudely, often with increasing irritation, to someone hovering between certainty and uncertainty. What does it matter if you make the wrong decision, or take the wrong road? Life is all experience, all discovery—at least it should be. 'Make up your mind!' I told myself, severely, when I began to dither this way and that, and immediately the decision was made, I felt better.

So now I knew, quite definitely, that I had to fill this waiting period between the chapters of life, with the children's articles. I could foresee another battle at the Ministry of Labour, and a long report on my case, in triplicate, for there appeared no scarcity of paper at the Ministries. The job at the Ministry that had seemed interesting and varied a year ago, had become nothing more than a tedious repetition. Only very rarely did we see or hear anything more disturbing than that a shipment of raw materials had arrived at a certain port, or that Base Number 17 had received a consignment of these same raw materials at 21 hours on the 18th instant. Such data could become extremely boring over a long period, to young women like myself, who had never yet seen either the raw material or the finished article.

'Why don't they send us on a visit to an aircraft factory, then we should be much more interested in our job?' I had suggested one day of the Departmental Chief.

'Not a bad idea—we must see about it.' he answered, politely, but nothing came of it, for everyone was much too busy with the war.

'Square pegs in round holes' was my main impression of my colleagues both at County Hall and the Ministry of Aircraft

Production. The waste of potential *human* raw material was appalling! My interest quickly flagged when I was expected to be nothing more than a mechanical instrument of some vast organisation, a small cog in a huge wheel, a nonentity. The individual was swamped in officialdom, red tape and lethargy. Enthusiasm was definitely discouraged. It was a nuisance. You conformed to pattern or got out—on the strength of a doctor's certificate! Only this precious scrap of paper could release you now from 'directed employment'. I rather enjoyed a battle with authority, and I was determined to get out of London as soon as possible.

*　　*　　*　　*　　*

'Nervous exhaustion'—I smiled as I read the doctor's diagnosis, and remembered Rosie, the last time I had sat in this same waiting room.

'We all got it now, ducks, this nervous exhaustion, makes yer laugh, don't it?'

Yes, Rosie, it did make me laugh, for there was nothing more seriously wrong than the frequent attacks of migraine I had known for the past ten years. But the little scrap of paper was my passport to the country. Not even the haughty counter clerk at the Ministry of Labour could denounce it, and I pushed it across the counter with some bravado.

'Where would you like to go?' he asked, surprisingly. 'We have a good choice of aircraft factories, all buried in the country, and all begging for personnel.'

'Good gracious!' I stuttered. 'That's a nice change. I mean—I thought I had to be *directed*?'

'Oh no, not any more. You may choose,' he insisted, graciously. 'Will you step into the office, and I will get our Mr Smith to show you the files.'

Then he smiled, disarmingly, and turned his attention to the next applicant. It was rather like the game we played in the 'Infants' at the Village School—'Eeny, meeny, miny, mo'—and I felt like closing my eyes and jabbing the list with a finger.

'*All* aircraft factories?' I asked.

'*All* aircraft factories,' Mr Smith replied—every bit as courteous as that nice counter clerk.

'And all in the country?'

'All in the country,' he echoed.

I scanned the list eagerly. Many of the names were familiar to me now, and one in particular, stood out prominently.

'Westhill Aircraft Company. I'm familiar with that one,' I told Mr Smith excitedly.

'Really?' his raised eyebrows questioned my right to be familiar with an organisation employing some sixteen thousand workers. 'Then perhaps, you would like to go to Somerset, Miss Shears?'

'Yes, I should,' I decided, with my usual impetuosity, and he looked very pleased with me, and began to make notes on a form, and to fill in details. 'How soon can I leave my London job?' I interrupted.

'Are you paid monthly?'

'Yes.'

'Then you give a month's notice.'

'Thank you! That's not long to wait, is it?'

His grey head lifted from the desk, and now I could see his eyes were tired, and he was no longer young.

'It's no time at all, when you have something to look forward to. I quite envy you,' he said and finished the form. Then he filled in another, much smaller, and with only a few particulars of my last employment, and reason for leaving. 'You will get a free travel warrant, Miss Shears. I will give it to you now.'

'Thank you very much!' I was quite overwhelmed by his generosity.

'Now this form you hand it to the Personnel Manager of the Westhill Aircraft Company, together with the doctor's certificate. Is that clearly understood?'

'Perfectly, thank you.'

We both stood up, exchanged smiles and a polite handshake.

'Goodbye—good luck!' he called after me.

*　　*　　*　　*　　*

As soon as I started on the articles, I realised it was a medium I should enjoy, and I wondered why I hadn't written for children before. Only two of the articles ever appeared in print, because the magazine ceased publication a few months later, owing to the restrictions of paper and printing in wartime. But I was unaware of this misfortune at the time of writing, and devoted two hours each morning to their composition.

'When the war is over I shall write a book for children,' I told Mother importantly—home for the week-end, and feeling rather pleased with myself. 'I shall use a Biblical background and have Biblical characters,' I enlarged on the idea, with enthusiasm. 'The Old Testament is rich in material and it has the most marvellous characters. I still read Grandmother's Bible, you know. Would you allow me to have Father's travelling clock? You will never use it, will you, because you never travel. For some unaccountable reason I can't wear a wrist watch—at least, I *can* wear it, but it either gains half-an-hour, or stops altogether!'

'I'm not surprised,' said Mother, quite unconcerned by this monologue. She was making one of her usual cakes, and since the recipe had not changed since she had her first kitchen back in the year 1905, she could also keep an eye on her young grandson, who was sitting under the kitchen table with a hand-made 'garage'—one of Henry's masterpieces—and a collection of matchboxes, to represent toy cars. Mother was still a great believer in invention and imagination, and her grandson was expected to use both, as his father before him. Costly and elaborate toys were never provided—or expected! The small boy, so like his grandfather, was playing quite contentedly with the matchboxes, and only came up for air when his grandmother put the cake in the oven.

'Can I scrape the bowl now, Gran?' he asked, eagerly.

She looked at him with love and with pride—her first grandchild! Pushing a lock of curly, auburn hair out of his eyes, she kissed his freckled cheek, and gave him the wooden spoon.

'When the war is over will be time enough to decide about the writing,' she said, her mind on the child. 'Everything will return to normal then. Yes, you may have your Father's clock.'

*   *   *   *   *

Now that I was leaving them, forever, I became quite attached to the Zolameks and the Professor, almost on terms of intimacy with Mrs P and Miss Bennet, and the Colonel actually invited me to supper one evening!

Mama Zolamek, grievously disappointed when the baby stayed in Suffolk, had nevertheless quite shaken off her despondency, and had offered her services as a teacher at a school for Jewish children.

As for dear Katie O'Brien, she burst into a flood of tears when I told her I was leaving, and declared, passionately,

'I shall be handing in me notice at Easter, for there's nothing but a broken heart to be enjoying now, with all me favourite tenants leaving the place!'

I was sad to leave her and the child, for we had shared so many hours of joy and anxiety in her basement room. Neither of us could be unhappy for long, and shared laughter is as precious as shared sorrow. I took them both out to Lyons Corner House for a 'high tea' to soften the blow, and we promised to keep in touch with the usual disregard for circumstances. I could feel quite an affection for the dreary apartment house, now that the time had come to leave it, and excused all manner of inconveniences we had endured during the worst days of the blitz.

Katie, I knew, was more disturbed by the vacant top floor than anything Hitler could send over!

'Likely as not some more Foreigners will be wanting lodgings and I shall fill up the empty rooms with *Poles*!' Katie told me, defiantly, as the taxi door closed. It was a fitting epitaph.

We did not meet again, and letter-writing, for Katie, was torment. She answered my first two letters, then carried on the fitful correspondence for several years with an elaborate Christmas card, in which she signed herself, 'Yours truly, K. O'Brien.'

5

SOMERSET

The familiar emptiness of my heart and mind on parting with family or friends, accompanied me on the long journey to Somerset. The two fibre suitcases, after so many journeys, were looking rather shabby and battered, and I staggered under their weight down Platform One at Paddington Station. Porters seemed to have vanished completely into the war machine, and young uniformed service men and women pushed heavy trucks piled with their luggage, and thought it a huge joke.

The station was seething with a mixed crowd of service personnel and civilians. We queued for refreshments in the dingy buffet, then stood, shoulder to shoulder, to drink it, our luggage piled in untidy heaps against the walls. The almost total absence of children reminded me that the second evacuation from London had been more effective that the first, and few had returned.

I no longer envied the group of Wrens in their smart uniforms for I realised now they were even more subject to 'direction' and 'disciplinary action' than civilians. Their superior officers were drinking sherry at the bar, in company with two naval officers. They were all behaving with that special decorum befitting the Senior Service. The taller of the two men, in profile, had an extraordinary likeness to my adored Third Mate, and my heart plunged for a split second. But when he turned his head I could see that his eyes were grey and he hadn't the same distinction. To some woman—perhaps to one of the Wren officers—he would appear to be distinctive, but not to me. But such comparisons were stupid, and it was time to forget this romantic attachment to an image.

I sat on my suitcases in the corridor, as far as Swindon, then slipped into a vacant seat. This mode of travel was customary now, and the corridors were as packed as the carriages. The noticeable hush, as we jerked uncomfortably out of Paddington Station, was felt in every part of the train, for it was the quietness of anguished hearts at parting, and the sudden realisation of the appalling havoc all around us. Seen in the familiar areas of our daily lives, we had grown accustomed to ruins, gaping walls, and windowless houses, but here, from the window of the train, we saw the awful panorama of destruction—the yawning craters in the back gardens, where once householders had grown cabbages and Canterbury bells, the rows of little houses that had crumbled into huge mounds of bricks and twisted metal, the heaps of rubble.

A middle-aged woman, who sat beside me on a folding camp stool, stared vacantly into the distance, beyond the ruins. She had already explained, before the train started, that since she had not slept for three nights, she would be poor company on the journey, but perhaps I would excuse her if she dozed a little on the way? She was a widow, whose only son, a navigator attached to a squadron at Biggin Hill, had been shot down, and reported missing from a raid on Hamburg. She had been on a visit to her sister at Putney, and was on her way back to her home at Swindon, where she worked in a factory, manufacturing chemicals. All the anguish of a mother's forlorn heart was there, in her tired eyes, and the droop of her head. But she was brave and calm, for life had taught her patience and fortitude in the other war, when she had lost the father of her son. As she gazed out of the window, I knew that she saw nothing but the splintered body of the aircraft, spinning towards the sea, and her son falling into space.

Her courage had the same quality of endurance as Mother's—her face held the same grave blend of shyness and reserve. She would never burden anyone with her private hell, for having told me, in the simplest way possible, why she must have a little doze, she proceeded to do so. With her shoulder touching mine, I could share the weight of her weary body, but not the burden of her grief. Her hands were folded quietly over the silk scarf she had removed from her aching head. Her brown hair was streaked with grey.

Compassion flooded my own self-pity, and I was ashamed.

Why should I be spared a little suffering, when it was born entirely of my own indiscretions? My companion had lost her entire family—husband and son—not merely parted from them for a few short months. I thought of all the families who would never be reunited in this world.

My faith in the ultimate unity was still unshaken by doubt. I had read no theological dogma, but Grandmother's Bible was still in my luggage. The Resurrection of Jesus seemed to my simple philosophy sufficient proof of immortality. The spirit of man, after three days, would be as aware of life and death as Jesus—the only living example of the Resurrection. I believed profoundly in life after death, and the survival of the personality. Grandmother's Bible, in my luggage, was as widely read as the Oxford Dictionary given me by 'Uncle John,' my first love. The worn covers were proof of my affection for both!

*   *   *   *   *

'It's all in the lap of the Gods!', one of my three companions declared airily, as we bumped along in the local bus towards our destination. The conductor, at first sight, had refused to allow us aboard with all our suitcases, but one of the men informed him that we were on our way to serve our King and Country in a *bloody aircraft factory*!

I blinked at this first introduction to factory life, and climbed aboard with my baggage. I was getting rather tired of dragging it around, and as anxious as the rest to get settled down in our new quarters. The men, it seemed, were better informed on the question of accommodation. Private lodgings had all been snapped up months ago, and all new recruits were obliged to live at the hostel, half a mile from the factory. A thousand workers were housed there, men and women.

The hostel, according to my informant, had a communal canteen, a dance hall, also used as a cinema, a shop and a BAR!

'They can keep all the rest, so long as they've got a bloody bar!' said the blasphemous one, pushing his cap to the back of his head.

We tumbled out of the bus at the factory gates, and stood on the tarmac, like four refugees, surrounded by our bags. Then we lined up to show our credentials to a uniformed guard on the gate. They were taking no chances here, apparently, with suspicious-looking characters who might turn out to be agents for the Gestapo!

'Okay, you lot. Report at the office marked 'Personnel'.

I was being 'directed' again, and my heart sank at the prospect of working in this vast, ugly camouflaged prison.

'May I leave my luggage here? I can't carry it any further,' I declared emphatically.

The guard looked me over with fresh interest. I was wearing the new hat at a jaunty angle, and was not too crumpled after the long train journey.

He grinned assent, and tossed my cases into his little sentry box.

The men who had travelled with me on the bus were already in line for interview. We had all become so queue-conscious since the war, even if only three people waited for attention they automatically stood one behind the other. I sat down to wait, on the only available chair, with a nonchalant air.

I was pleasantly surprised again, as I had been at the Ministry of Labour, by the cordiality of the man who greeted me, from a small desk in a small office. There was nothing intimidating about his manner, or his headquarters, and we exchanged a smile as well as a handshake, before settling down to a long discourse on the various vacancies.

'Shall you like working in a factory with a whole lot of other people?' he asked.

'Not very much,' I confessed. 'But it's what I came for, and there is no alternative, is there?'

'Well, as a matter of fact, there is, but it's a domestic job, and you have been accustomed to clerical work, according to your papers.' He flicked the pages of a file on his desk.

'I'm prepared to try anything!' I told him.

'But this is a housemaid's job at the hostel. The housekeeper asked me to send along someone suitable.'

His twinkling eyes focused on the new hat and the white gloves—I had taken the precaution to carry them in my bag on the journey.

'I'm very suitable!' I insisted.

'All right, it's up to you, and it shouldn't be too difficult to get transferred to an office job, after three months, if the other is too hard. You won't like the look of the hostel, any more than you like the look of this place. Everyone groans with dismay when they first arrive, but it's not so bad, once you get used to it, and forget the outside ugliness. There is a friendly atmosphere here, anyway, and a mixed bunch of workers from all over the British Isles—Welsh miners, Irish labourers, housewives from Scotland, retired Army Majors, and youngsters straight from school. It should be interesting and amusing.

'I'm prepared to find it so,' I told him. 'Can you give me any details about this housemaid's job at the hostel?'

'Yes, I have it here. "Housemaids to be responsible for one block of furnished rooms, and thirty residents—for cleaning their rooms, changing linen, and generally maintaining a homely atmosphere. Residents should make their own beds. Housemaids are required to wear white overalls. Hours of duty —8 am to 5 pm, Sundays free. Wages 50 shillings weekly, plus full board and lodgings." '

'I like the bit about maintaining a homely atmosphere! You can put me down as a housemaid, please!'

He laughed, filled in another form for the file and handed me a chit of introduction to the Housekeeper.

'Good luck! Go easy on the scrubbing, and send in the next applicant,' he told me.

In the outer office, more applicants had formed themselves into a queue.

The sun was shining now as I marched back to the gates to collect my bags and await transport to the hostel. My companions of the bus were also waiting and discussing the jobs they had been allocated.

'Bloody unskilled fitters!' muttered the blasphemous one, a cigarette dangling from his sulky mouth.

'What did they offer you, Miss?' asked the quiet man, as we climbed into the van.

'A housemaid's job at the hostel,' I laughed. 'Actually I chose it.'

As the blasphemous one opened his mouth to swear, I stopped him—'All right, don't say it!' Then he let out a raucuous laugh instead.

The hostel was hideously ugly—a collection of two-storey buildings, divided by new roads and areas of rough grass. The main buildings, separated from the workers' accommodation, were a little more dignified, but the whole place suggested a prisoner-of-war camp.

'Report at Reception!' we were told, and my bags were dropped on the pavement beside me.

The men hurried indoors, but I stood for a few moments, looking about me, and my enquiring gaze travelled out and beyond the ugly buildings, to the surrounding hills.

The air was fresh and clean. It was incredibly quiet and peaceful in the mid-afternoon lull, and I could smell beef roasting for the evening meal.

When I had reported at Reception, I was sent to find the Housekeeper in the linen room.

Mrs McIntyre was a grey-haired, forthright woman from Aberdeen, with a grown-up family, and a husband serving in North Africa. Immaculate in a starched white overall, she looked very efficient, I thought, and also quite capable of dealing with all the problems of female staff in war time. But she was glancing doubtfully at my small, tailored figure. I was tired, and a little annoyed by the assumption that one had to weigh about twelve stone, and dress like an abandoned orphan, in order to be considered a useful addition to the war effort.

'You look a wee bit on the frail side? Had you no thought of doing clerical work?' she asked anxiously, from behind a counter piled with clean sheets.

'I'm not at all frail, Mrs McIntyre, and I was offered clerical jobs by the Personnel Officer, but decided on the housemaid job.'

Her stern features relaxed into a smile.

'Well, it's nice to meet someone who can make up her mind so quickly. Take off your hat, now, and sit you down.'

I snatched off my hat and gloves, and sank thankfully on to a chair beside the counter.

'It's changing day for half the hostel on Monday, and the rest on Wednesday,' Mrs McIntyre explained. 'Thirty beds every week will seem an awful lot of beds, when you start on the job, but you haven't to change them all in one day, you know, and I suggest you do upstairs one day, and downstairs the next. I am putting you on Block Number Eight, and that's all men. Most of them will make their beds, but the lazy ones will get out of it. Each man has a clean sheet, pillow case and towel every week. On changing days you do no cleaning, only tidy as you go round the block. Most of the men on your block are reasonably tidy, but, of course, you get the exceptions, as you do in every family. Your biggest offenders will be the three we call the 'dirty tykes'—Bill West, Taffy Williams and Joe Finlay. They will go to bed in their boots if you let them! But don't let them get away with it. Put your foot down from the start, or you will find yourself with a pigsty.'

'Start as you mean to continue—as my mother would say,' I murmured.

'Exactly. My last girl was much too easy-going, by far, but she hadn't any interest in the job and got a transfer to the factory. She's happier on a machine, I believe. It requires less energy and initiative. There is plenty of scope for initiative here, Sarah, and I don't want you to think it's going to be plain drudgery. It depends entirely on your attitude and your way of tackling it. If you can see it as I see the job—useful, worthwhile, and essential to the comfort and happiness of thirty men deprived of family and home life—then you'll be content. Some of the men have been living here for two years already, and I have been here since the start.'

'But that's exactly how I *do* see it, or I shouldn't be here,' I told her.

'That's the girl!' she laughed, and patted my shoulder. 'With good method, plenty of common sense, and a whole lot of tolerance, it's not so bad. Now I'll show you round your block before the residents get back from the factory. Your own little single room is on the same block, so you should feel more at home.'

We each picked up a suit case, and walked away from the main building towards the residents' quarters.

'Why blocks?' I asked her, curiously. 'It's such an ugly name.'

'It's an ugly place, until you look over there,' she indicated the hills in the distance. 'Lovely walks, if you like walking. And a bluebell wood just beyond the orchard, near the top gate.'

Bluebells! Perhaps I could pick a few to decorate the bare little rooms I could see through the open windows? What would Bill, Taffy and Joe make of a housemaid who scattered bluebells around the place? Already I was planning to beg some empty jam jars from the catering department, quite unaware that the jam came in tins, weighing 28 lbs apiece— red pulp and yellow pulp alternately!

We went first to the only single room on the block—*my* room! It was like a nun's cell, bare, clean and modest, with a partition dividing it into two cubicles—for sleeping and sitting. The only luxury was an electric fire, which we were permitted to use from October till May. In my new expansive mood I was feeling maternal, and could see myself in this little room, surrounded by a family of men, all expecting to be mothered! But I could tell too that this job was going to take all my physical strength—the stone floors, for example, would have to be wet-mopped.

'There is only one empty bed on your block at the moment, in the Major's room, so I hope they will send us someone who will fit in with the old boy. He's one of the old school, and keeps his room meticulously clean and tidy. He will change his own linen, so that's one less for you! If they send us another tough guy we shall have to do a bit of very discreet manoeuvring— but we shall see. The new man should be here next week-end. Well, there it is, Sarah—your domain! Do the best you can with it. Now I'll leave you to unpack, and make yourself at home. Staff supper at 6 o'clock, breakfast at 7.30, and on duty at 8!'

Standing in the doorway of my room, I was aware of the same incredible quietness I had noticed on arrival. It was very soothing to nerves and senses, so long accustomed to noise. But apart from the heavenly quiet, I felt already, in this strange environment, that I had to come here, that I belonged here now, and would stay for a very long time. 'Someone to need me —someone to love'—yes, all thirty of them! In making a home for thirty men I could also make a home for myself.

*   *   *   *   *

I hadn't even started unpacking my cases when the afternoon quietness and peace was suddenly disturbed by a crowd of workers flocking in the main gate. The majority seemed to be in a desperate hurry to reach the canteen, but a few dispersed to the blocks, and I could see several men coming across the road towards Block Number Eight.

Now that I had to confront them I was seized with shyness and confusion. Twenty-nine strange men and another at the week-end! How on earth should I cope? Then I reminded myself, sternly, that I hadn't to get involved in personal relationships and there would be no complications. My original idea of 'mothering' them was still the best. Thirty men should not present so great a problem as three, I reasoned. I must have no favourites in my large family of men. That was something else I had to guard against.

This new sense of responsibility was very satisfying in the quiet seclusion of my little room, but now I had to shake off the shyness and go out to meet them, or they would be unaware of my existence till the morning, and then, with the rush of early breakfast (6.30 for the residents), they would not care to be bothered. Mrs Mac had told me the men only came back to the block to wash or to sleep. They would spend the evening in the bar, watching a film, playing cards or billiards, but always in a crowd. The lone individual was rare and considered rather odd and anti-social.

With assumed casualness I waited at the front door to introduce myself. Six dusty, tired men, in dark shirts and dungarees, stumbled across the rough grass towards me. Suddenly I hadn't to pretend any more. Shyness and nervousness disappeared in the one overwhelming sense of maternity. This is how Mother felt greeting her children from school, I thought—and my smile was warm and genuine, not artificial.

'Hullo! I'm Sarah—your new housemaid!' I announced brightly.

They stopped dead on the cinder-track and looked me over with dull eyes.

Only one spoke 'So what?' he drawled.

They couldn't care less, apparently.

It was something of a shock, and I stepped aside to let them pass. They clattered noisily down the stone passage and a shout of laughter floated back to me. Tears pricked my eyes. It was silly to be so dismayed for they were tired and bad-tempered. Men never could hide their feelings like women, I reminded myself. Tomorrow they would probably be quite civil, and completely unaware they had badly shaken my confidence and enthusiasm. Now I had to force myself to stay there, for the urge to retire to the privacy of my own room was very strong.

A tall, upright figure, in a dark suit and trilby hat, had detached himself from a group and was walking towards me. This must be the Major, I thought.

'How do you do, I'm Sarah, your new housemaid,' I began, tentatively.

He also stopped dead on the cinder-track and looked me

over with bland disinterest, shifting his rolled umbrella from the right to the left arm. Raising his hat he murmured,

'How do you do, I'm Major Jackson-Clarke.'

From the tip of his polished boots to the top of his smooth iron-grey head, he was every inch a military man. A small moustache covered his upper lip.

'I trust you will like it here, and not find the work too arduous. I make my own bed, and change my own linen. You will find my room needs very little attention,' he told me.

'Thank you,' I murmured, politely, feeling like a chamber-maid.

I stepped aside, and he went in, bristling with importance. Then suddenly it all seemed rather funny and my next approach was more forceful.

'Hullo, boys! I'm Sarah, the new housemaid, so you had better watch out!'

The three men stopped, stared and grinned sheepishly. They all wore dirty caps and they looked like tramps.

'You wouldn't be Bill, Taffy and Joe—would you?' I asked, innocently.

'That's us,' said the big man, spitting on his hand and wiping it down his corduroys. His grip nearly broke my fingers, and his wide grin was so infectious I found myself laughing. 'I'm Bill—this chap 'ere is Joe, and this little twerp is our Taff.'

'Evening, Miss,' muttered Joe and Taffy respectfully.

'Sarah,' I reminded them.

'Sarah,' they all three repeated, dutifully.

Well, if these were an example of my 'dirty tykes', I much preferred them to the Major. But I had to be careful to treat them all fairly.

'I shall need your help and co-operation, for I've had no experience of this kind of work,' I began.

'You don't want to worry, Miss Sarah,' Bill interrupted. 'We don't give no trouble at all when we *likes* a person, see? It's only when they send us a snobbish little bitch we turn nasty,' he explained, reasonably. Joe nodded agreement, and Taffy commented mournfully,

'It's here we are and here we have to stay for the duration, sure to goodness.'

'Cheer up Taffy!' I coaxed, 'I'm not a bit snobbish, and I'm very happy to be here, but I'm a little bit nervous of not keeping up to schedule. It would help, tremendously, if you would all make your beds.'

'Anything to oblige,' Bill agreed magnanimously. 'After all you're only a little bit of a thing, aren't you? The last one was pretty hefty, wasn't she Taff?'

'Aye, but she hadn't a thought in her head only to get finished and off to the pictures with the boy-friend,' sang Taffy in his sad Welsh voice.

'Here come some more of my residents!' I told them, looking towards another group, swarming across the road.

'Residents!' scoffed Joe, 'A bunch of Irish hooligans, can't trust 'em! Eating out of your hand one minute, and wanting to murder you the next!'

'Yes, indeed man,' said Taffy mournfully, going indoors.

The Irish were young and gregarious. Their honeyed voices melted like Kate O'Brien's, as they greeted me effusively. Their smiles were innocently deceptive, as they slipped past with the sly, slinking movements of cats in the long grass. When the rest had disappeared up the stone stairs, the youngest hovered, then crept back, to ask disarmingly,

'Will ye be coming to the flicks with me tonight?'

'Not tonight, but thank you for inviting me,' I said.

His eyes flickered over me, then he shrugged, pouting with disappointment,

'So—please yourself!'

He followed his companions up the stairs—leaping three steps in a single bound, like a child, showing off his cleverness. My heart melted with a new understanding of their wildness and youth, in this restricted place.

After the meal in the canteen, groups of men drifted across the road, and I greeted them all in turn: twenty-nine men, from all walks of life, living under the same roof. Rough voices shouted obscene jokes from the lavatories, water splashed in all the bathrooms, somebody was yelling 'Roll out the Barrel', and the Major was taking some washing from the line.

It was bedlam, at the moment, but soon they would be dispersed over the hostel. This was our home for better or worse, for the war's duration—three months or three years? As Taffy would say, in his singing voice, 'It's here we are and here we have to stay, sure to goodness!'

I found most of the housemaids at supper in the canteen. They were as mixed a bunch as the residents—Irish, Welsh, Scots, North Country, West Country, and Cockneys—ranging in age from seventeen to seventy! Several were still on duty, clearing up after their night-shift workers who slept during the day, I was told by a plump little housewife from Bethnal Green.

'You'll find some of your night-shift chaps in bed tomorrow. They don't have to be disturbed, so we have to do our work quietly and not clatter about.'

While she was chatting to me, at the end of the long trestle table, I had an opportunity to look around this big, communal canteen, where meals were served in relays, according to the day and night shifts. The benches were partly emptied now, for most of the workers had dispersed to their blocks, or gone straight to the bar. The women and girls were probably changing their clothes for the evening entertainment. Dirty crockery and plates of unfinished food were scattered over the bare tables, waiting for the trolley girls to collect. The roast beef that smelt so savoury, three hours ago, was not so appetising in pools of cold gravy. There seemed to be an awful lot of waste to my frugal mind, so long accustomed to small rations.

I had collected my own meal on a tin tray from the service counter, but had to force myself to eat in surroundings of such appalling disorder. Perhaps this was just another aspect of communal living that one had to accept? My neighbour seemed undeterred by it.

'Will you excuse me, Nellie? I have to unpack,' I asked politely, for it seemed that we would be sitting there for the rest of the evening.

She gave me an old-fashioned look, and said crossly,

'Nobody asks to be excused here, my girl, you just get up and go.'

So I got up and went!

Still postponing my unpacking until later in the day, I felt an urge to explore the country lanes in the vicinity of the hostel, and to rid myself of the disagreeable odours of the canteen! I knew that I had to be one of the few individualists who would cling, tenaciously, to a few hours of privacy, and that I should have to be ready to defend my right to do so. It had happened before, in earlier chapters of my life, so would be no new experience, I thought dispassionately, for I was tired now,

after the long eventful day, and could only think dispassionately. All my working day would be devoted to my large family
of men, and I was already prepared to enjoy my work here as I
had never enjoyed my work in London. Mealtimes, with Nellie
at my elbow, would have to be endured, with a good grace.
But then I had to escape from the crowd—to be alone. An
aching head and weary limbs would find relaxation only in the
quiet countryside. On Sundays, when no work was expected
of me, I could climb the hills, or explore the Cotswold villages
by bus.

The two widely different spheres of crowded community and
solitary isolation, I soon discovered, were divided by nothing
more substantial than a five-barred gate. I climbed it easily,
for it was padlocked, and dropped down on the other side, into
a small orchard of matured apple trees, already in blossom.
The grass was fresh and green, and a narrow pathway led to a
stile. Here, in this quiet place, was no pretence—I could be
myself. Rootless, I could feel the roots holding me, and the old
trees in the orchard embracing me with their twisted arms.
Now I was Mother's daughter, and Father was lost to me. He
didn't belong here.

*   *   *   *   *

I woke to the tapping of the night-watchman on all the doors,
and his gruff voice calling out to the boys—

'Six o'clock! Time to get up!'

I could imagine their reactions, curses and grumbles, as they
tumbled reluctantly out of their warm beds. The Major would
probably be first in the bathroom, filling his big enamel jug
with hot water for shaving.

Fully awake, as always, the instant my eyelids flickered open,
I wished I had a kettle to boil, but it was wishful thinking. If I
hurried, though, there was still time to beat the breakfast queue
in the canteen, and I could fill my thermos flask with tea from
the big urn on the service counter. Slipping out through the
boiler room, to avoid any contact with any of my sleepy or
bad-tempered men, the sense of being in the right place and in
the right job was still with me. The eagerness and enthusiasm
was still there, and the fresh, invigorating air from the surrounding hills added to my sense of well-being. It was almost the
same feeling of dedication I had experienced on my first voyage,

when the children developed measles, and were lying in rows on the nursery floor, 'somebody to need me, someone to love.'

The need to love was more compelling now than the need to be loved. Values change. But I was still desperately afraid of getting involved again, with one particular man, and avoided it at all costs, for the last involvement had been a shattering experience. The enormity of my foolishness, that night, in Bombay, still haunted me. I would always remember how I had been shown then that sex was not a subject to experiment with because I lacked knowledge, but a force to be reckoned with, in any man as strong and virile as the one who had sent me away—untouched. Physical attraction, I had discovered that night, had a natural magnetism that defied all the conventions. Only the timely intervention of the man's self discipline had prevented an act of sexual violence that could have ruined my attitude to sex for the rest of my life.

But now, on this fresh morning in the country, with a brave new chapter opening, I was happy with my big family of men.

'Safety in numbers, my girl!' Nellie had reminded me, as we drank our cocoa together in the canteen last night.

*　　*　　*　　*　　*

In a clean starched overall, I started on the bedrooms at the far end of the block, and found most of the boys had made their beds by the simple process of pulling the quilt over the tumbled bedclothes. I had to remake them all in anticipation of Mrs Mac's inspection, but obviously they had done their best for me on my first morning, and I was touched by their co-operation. Only the tough guys in Number Five and Six, had departed for work with a careless disregard of the new housemaid. Unmade beds, scattered boots, and empty beer bottles greeted me, as I pushed open the doors. A line of washing was strung across one corner, and shrunken socks, vests and pants dripped pools of water on the floor.

They would have to be reprimanded, I thought in disgust, for they were turning their part of the block into a slum. Anger flamed in me, as I tossed the dirty mats out of the window, and the washing into the bath. Cigarette stubs littered the floors. But when I had swept and tidied, and dashed around with a wet-mop and a bucket of soapy water, the transformation was so rewarding, my indignation turned towards forgiveness!

Nevertheless, my physical strength was momentarily exhausted by mid-morning tea-break.

'You want to go easy on them cement floors for a week or two, my girl. No sense in wearing yourself out for that lot!' said Nellie, as I sank into a chair beside her.

'They can't be worse than my lot in Number Nine and Ten,' said Edie, defensively. 'They got the worst reputation in the place, them four have. Been reported to the Management more than once, but what do they care? They know they won't be kicked out, because they're *skilled*, see? They got a shop steward to keep an eye on things. Get away with murder, all them skilled chaps do. They think they're the cats' whiskers!'

'Give me the *unskilled* chaps, any day,' said Rosie, who was nearly seventy, and liked her Guinness for supper. Cocoa, she had declared, last night, would rot her boots!

'Two a penny, they are, luv, the unskilled chaps, and all shapes and sizes like a jar of mixed pickles! I've got two retired school teachers, three ex-policemen, a couple of bricklayers, a road sweeper and a half-a-dozen railway porters on my block, and all unskilled fitters in the blinkin' factory for the duration!'

Outside, the roads were deserted, and I hurried back to work, with only a cursory glance at the distant hills. With the tough guys' washing blowing on the clothes line at the back of the block, and a dozen mats lined up for brushing on the grass verge in front, I gave myself up to an orgy of cleaning. A strong smell of Jeyes disinfectant pervaded the place.

'You're flooding the place!' said a disgruntled night-shift resident, padding barefoot to the bathroom. 'And you don't have to use Lysol, you know, we're not all that dirty!'

* * * * *

'Changing days' were a nightmare to all of us, even the strongest. There was no trolley or transport of any kind to help us distribute the heavy piles of clean linen or return the bundles of dirty linen to Mrs Mac's department for checking. We each collected our own clean linen, after breakfast, and trudged, staggering under the weight, down the tarmac road, across the rough grass, and along the cinder tracks.

'You're darn lucky, my girl, your block's not more than 300 yards from the linen room. Me and Glad and Edie got to walk about a half mile to that top lot near the orchard!' Nellie reminded me, truculently.

Could it really be only 300 yards? It seemed to me, that first week, that I should be defeated—not by the men or the hard cleaning but the simple process of 'changing days'.

But again, I found the results of my hard labour so rewarding that the misery of a breaking back was nothing, as compared to the pleasure of counting twenty-nine spotlessly clean beds—the changing spread over two days, at Mrs Mac's suggestion.

It was on the evening of the second day that I had to find peace and relaxation again in the country beyond the hostel, though my aching limbs and throbbing head cried out for bed. Climbing wearily over the gate, I sauntered slowly across the orchard, and over the stile to the wood. Squeezing through a gap in the hedge, the trees closed in around me, and almost immediately I was refreshed and comforted by their embracing presence. The smell of wet earth was, for me, always evocative of childhood, and all the simplicity of our pleasures and pastimes—when we searched for nothing more exciting than the first primrose, or the nest of the skylark (which we never found) or the biggest black-heart cherry in the orchard.

It was evocative, too, of Mother's whole attitude to life and to her children, for she was an earthy person, born and bred in a small, stone farmhouse, surrounded by furrowed fields, and age-old timbered barns where waggons and sacks of grain were the only toys she ever knew. The smell of wet earth to me, her restless and rebellious daughter, had the power to check my thoughts, and divert my wandering feet into paths of quiet relaxation and peace. I stopped, instinctively, took a deep breath, and inhaled the taste of the wood, for it tasted of mushrooms, moss and mildew. The miracle of an early spring had draped the naked branches in fresh foliage. The silver birches, slender, graceful and rather aloof, reached upwards to the sky away from the stolid, sturdy oaks, and the spreading arms of the beeches. Birds twittered in the twilight, and the stillness was broken only by the snapping of twigs underfoot, and the harsh screeching of a pheasant.

A carpet of bluebells covered the area most thickly wooded, and I began to gather the biggest bunch I could carry, while the sticky sap from the hollow stems stained my fingers. Fifteen empty paste jars stood waiting on the window sill in my room. The men will be delighted, I thought, to find bluebells decorating their rooms tonight!

After spending more than an hour arranging the flowers in the little jars, and distributing them while the boys were absent, I waited, with my door ajar, at the end of the passage, for the reactions of those within earshot. The Major, always back at precisely ten o'clock, was the first to arrive. He went in, closed the door, opened it, and closed it again. Peeping round the corner, I saw the little jar of bluebells standing on the floor, nor *thrown* out, exactly, but *put* out. Why? Could it be that he had an aversion to bluebells, or simply that he disliked flowers in a bedroom.

'They use up the oxygen, nurse, and must be removed at night!'—my thoughts flew back to the ward in the big London hospital where I hung on to life by a slender thread at the age of fourteen. Poor old Major! I shot back to my room as heavy boots clattered in the front door, and Bill, Taffy and Joe ambled into their room.

'What's this 'ere?' followed a moment of groans and grunts as they collapsed on their beds.

'Bloody bluebells!' roared Bill, in disgust.

Then Taffy's singing voice piped up, mournfully.

'Is it the new girl now with a mind to turn us all into nice, refined gentlemen with flowers on the table—think you, bach?'

'But what can you *do* with bluebells?' Joe demanded anxiously—and slammed the door!

*   *   *   *   *

I stood in the doorway, that Saturday evening, waiting to welcome my 'new boy' to the family. I had bathed, washed my hair, and changed into a clean white overall and sandals. Bare-legged, cool, calm and collected, I wished he would hurry, for I wanted to be off to the woods again.

On the whole, I decided, it had been quite a successful week and even the bluebells had been appreciated by the most unlikely residents—the young Irish contingent, who had 'fallen over backwards', as Nellie would say, to thank me properly!

The sun was warm on my head and face—the long winter had passed. It was spring again!

Suddenly, I knew again that fatal sensation of being watched by someone whose very personality excited me. A man was striding across the rough grass towards me—a big, broad-shouldered, smiling man, with a fine strong head. He was wearing a dark tailored suit and bow tie, and a black homberg hat. He carried two large, expensive-looking suitcases. He was very assured, confident of a welcome, and he called out in a rich, jocular voice which was unmistakeably American,

'Hullo, there! I'm Paul Taylor! I was told to ask for Sarah.'

'I am Sarah.'

He dropped the cases at my feet, swept off his hat, and stood over me, overwhelmingly large and expansive. His lively dark eyes searched my burning cheeks, and held my own eyes in a long, unflickering stare.

Dismayed and shaken by the impact of this extraordinary person, I took his outstretched hand, then moved away, inviting him in, with a coolness that belied my trembling limbs. 'But this is ridiculous!' I told myself, as I hurried along to the Major's room, 'you can't feel it again! You mustn't! It's just the same physical attraction—nothing more. He is obviously a healthy, gregarious male, looking for someone to share his enjoyment of life in a backwater of rural Somerset.'

Striding purposefully into the bare, clean room, he dropped his bags on the vacant bed, and flung wide his arms, in a great, tearing sigh of relief. I stepped back quickly, well out of range of those spreading arms, and he grinned mischievously, tucked his hands in his trouser pockets, and looked around.

'Bluebells—for me?' he asked in that quick, decisive way I was beginning to find rather disconcerting.

'And the Major,' I reminded him, 'only he puts them out at night.'

'What on earth for?'

'I think he imagines they use up all the oxygen in the room?'

Paul Taylor flung back his head and roared. Great gusts of laughter spilled out of him, as it spilled out of Father, on the station platform, that memorable day, when he returned from the First World War. It was the same masculine, rip-roaring laugh, that had changed our quiet, orderly lives. But a man with such a laugh could also be rather alarming, if he had Father's unpredictable temperament. But this man hadn't got red hair and a waxed moustache. He was clean-shaven and rather pale with sparse greying hair.

Choking on a last gust of laughter, he declared, boisterously,

'But this is *marvellous*! This nice clean room, the bluebells, and the immediate prospect of meeting the delectable Major! Do you mind if I smoke?'

'Not at all,' I murmured, smiling secretly at the recollection of all the cigarette ends I had swept off the floors this week.

He was searching the shelf over the wash-basin—

'I was looking for an ash-tray,' he said.

'That's it, next to the Major's shaving brush—the cocoa tin lid,' I pointed out.

'Oh, I see—thanks.'

He tried to conceal the smile of amusement that trembled on his lips, but it spread irresistibly over his face, and engulfed me, in its warmth and gaiety.

'Will you excuse me?' I stammered. 'Staff supper is served punctually at six-thirty on Saturday.'

'Certainly.'

His candid eyes flickered over my bare legs, flushed cheeks and clean, shining hair.

'You look charming,' he said gently, and added, 'Thank you, Sarah, for the nice welcome and for the bluebells.'

Then he opened the door for me, and I slipped out, not daring to meet his eyes again.

Now I was really worried, for I had an awful feeling my new boy was going to be the biggest problem child in the entire family!

* * * * *

'Thank goodness he's fallen in step with the Major,' I thought, as I watched the two distinctive figures marching— there was no other word for it—down the cinder track, at precisely 6.25 am to join the queue for breakfast. I smiled with pride and pleasure at their striking appearance and their punctuality, for I knew they would cause a mild sensation together—one so tall and bristling with military precision, the other with his relaxed arrogance. They both wore dark suits and hats, and their shoes were highly polished. They carried dispatch cases, and gave the impression of urgent business awaiting their arrival at the factory. Deep in animated conversation, their cultured voices drifted back to me at the open window, most agreeably. But I mustn't let my pride in their distinction blunt my feelings for the rest, I reminded myself.

My 'tough guys' were getting more amenable, the Irish boys were naughty, but nice, and all were definitely improving in their dirty habits.

Little groups of men were drifting listlessly across the rough grass now, and I could see several of the cheeky youngsters from Edie's block, following the two immaculate figures at a safe distance, capering idiotically. It was rather like standing in the wings of a theatre, to watch the principle actors make their entry. Larger groups of men and women poured down the cinder tracks now, like the chorus of a grand opera! The wide open doors of the canteen swallowed them up. Doors banged in the block and heavy boots clattered down the stone stairways.

But who was Paul Taylor? And how would he fit into this pattern? I was curious to know more, but reluctant to ask too many direct questions. He might wish to remain anonymous? This would not be difficult in such a large community. One could have a private life entirely removed from the hostel and factory. It was not at all necessary to divulge anything but the few essential details demanded by the Ministry of Labour and the Management.

Nobody seemed in the least interested in me as a *person*, only as a worker. The main issue was work. The essential qualifications nothing more than a capacity to endure hard, laborious, routine work, for long hours. Whether employed in the factory or the hostel the same ruling applied. But you hadn't to become a mechanical unit at the hostel, and that was the only, and, to me, most important difference. It was entirely a matter for the individual whether she found, in the office, the kitchen, the canteen, or the blocks, a satisfaction and pride, or merely a dull and boring routine.

Paul Taylor and the Major, no less than the others, would be engulfed in the machine, as soon as they entered the factory gates. Yet, whatever their position—I could not see either of them as subordinates—they would keep that distinction and individuality.

My thoughts followed them, that morning, and wandered away from the crowded benches of women at our table. Nellie found my absent-mindedness a little irritating, for she was particularly voluble at breakfast time.

'Anything wrong?' she demanded.

'No—why?'

'I've told you twice already this bacon's so salt you'll need three cups of tea to wash it down!'

'I'm sorry, Nellie, but I hadn't noticed the bacon was salty.'

Nellie was always well informed. Over her second cup of tea she remarked casually,

'Your new chap arrived last night, I hear. Quite a swell, by all accounts. That makes two of them on your block, don't it? A pity, for you look like having trouble. They don't mix with the rest, and that makes for unpleasantness.'

'I don't see why it should be unpleasant,' I argued, defensively. 'After all the Major joins the boys for a drink in the bar, I understand, but that doesn't mean he has to spend the rest of the evening with them?'

Then, coaxingly, I asked her whether she had heard anything more about Paul Taylor—her young niece was working in the Reception Office.

'He's come to take over the Personnel Officer's job, at the factory.'

I tried to hide my pride and pleasure in my 'new boy' for I knew he was destined for something more than unskilled fitting!

'The other chap retires next week,' she added. 'Funny, though, to put a Yank on the job.'

But I was not interested in the other's man's retirement, only in Paul Taylor! Yet my interest must not be too obvious, for Nellie would broadcast her opinion all over the hostel, and Nellie's 'opinions' were forthright and often derogatory. But she couldn't resist the temptation to pass on all the titbits of information she gleamed from various sources, so I buttoned my impatience, and waited for more.

After she had dismissed the headlines of the morning paper as just so much propaganda, and was sipping her third cup of tea, she returned to the subject of the new resident.

'That new chap on your block, Sarah—he's been a Company Director, it seems. Redundant, I shouldn't wonder. What's the use of Company Directors when there's a war on? Got to come down to earth, those sort of chaps, and do something practical.'

'You're right, Nellie! You're absolutely right!' I told her. I then added casually, 'And do you know anthing more?'

'Yes, he's married,' she said. 'And got a kid, I think.'

My heart sank. The work was hard and exhausting that day, the bluebells fading. But I could not stop thinking about Paul Taylor, and I was eager, yet anxious to see him again.

They came back together—walking briskly, well ahead of the others, and the Major's umbrella still hung on his arm, in spite of the fine weather. Paul Taylor was still talking, and the topic must have been quite absorbing for they completely ignored the crowd of workers swarming in the gates behind them. I could see the Irish boys rushing for the bar—evidently their bacon had also been salty for breakfast! But Paul Taylor and the Major walked past both the bar and the canteen, and made straight for home!

A few minutes later I heard the hot water gurgling in the pipes in the boiler room, and Paul Taylor calling out to the Major that he was taking a bath. In less than half-an-hour he emerged, walking briskly back down the cinder track towards the canteen. He had changed into a grey flannel suit, and red-spotted bow tie. As he passed my window he was so close I could have touched him, and the urge to do so was strong and compelling. Then he ran into Bill, Joe and Taffy, a few yards from my window, and asked, bluntly,

'Is Sarah in the canteen?'

'No, she don't eat with us residents, she's *Staff*—is Sarah,' Bill explained.

'When does she eat?' Paul demanded.

Bill shrugged—'Can't say.' Then warming to the stranger, suggested mildly, 'Why not join us later, after you've had your grub? Sarah's promised to come to the flicks. It's Douglas Fairbanks, so it should be good—starts at seven in the main hall. Sit where you like for a bob!'

'Good Lord!' Paul Taylor exclaimed, with a wide grin. 'Thanks, I'll join you—and we will have a drink together after the show!' he called back boisterously.

They all turned slowly on their heels, to watch him stride across the road. Then Taffy, shrugging his thin shoulders declared dismally—

'I can't bear to watch him now, for he's too energetic for me at this time of the day.'

I came out from behind the curtain then, and called out to him as they went past,

'Never mind, Taffy dear, you can sleep on my shoulder all through the film, if you like!'

'You know something? I think that new bloke's fallen for you Sarah!' said Joe teasingly.

'Of course not, what an idea—he's only been here since yesterday evening!' I declared indignantly, and added as an afterthought, 'Besides, he's married.'

*　　*　　*　　*　　*

Was it because I had returned to my natural element, at last, that I found that month of May so enchanting? Or was it because Paul Taylor shared it?

He 'courted' me with old-world courtesy and a persistence that left no room for doubt. 'You see, I was right,' said Joe.

There seemed now, in this glorious month of May, to be two Paul Taylors—one who walked briskly down the cinder track in the early morning with the Major, and spent most of the evening in the bar, with the men—and another, who emerged fresh from his bath, glowing with warmth and an unexpected gentleness which was very comforting at the end of my long working day.

He made no secret of his preference for my company, and would take my hand, possessively, as we walked together to the top gate overlooking the orchard. This, for a whole month, had been the limit of our evening meetings. To lean on the gate, companionably, side by side, and breathe in the clean, sweet air from the hills. Pink and white blossom hung on the gnarled branches of the old trees, and wild parsley in the long grass was knee-deep, when I wandered there, alone, after Paul had left me, to join the Major in the bar.

Beyond the gate was still my own private territory, the orchard and the wood, that enchanted country I could not share with anyone, yet. These few acres, where I never once met any of the residents, and my own bedroom, was all that remained private in this communal place. I clung to them with a sort of desperation, as the last stronghold, linking me with the past, with the earthy roots of my maternal ancestry, and with the element of quietness so essential to me now.

Leaning on the gate, Paul smoked and talked, his voice lost its authoritative ring, and mellowed with the evening hour we spent together. Sometimes his strong hand would touch mine,

184

on the top bar of the gate, and my whole body trembled with this small contact. There had been a spark kindled between us, at that moment of meeting on the cinder track. But I told myself that it was never likely to flame into a dangerous fire, so long as we kept our rendezvous outdoors, and I was sensible.

Independence was still sweet, still to be preferred to the blasé associations of some couples, who made no secret of the fact that they slept together. Rules and regulations relating to the visiting hours, in the separate blocks of male and female residents, were blatantly ignored, and it was generally agreed that where one spent the night was one's own private affair.

Sensitive to this widespread clamour for a bed-mate, I shrank from exposing myself to the popular belief that no woman could remain a virgin for long under the pressure of such a predominantly male population! That Paul Taylor was aware of this, and trying to protect me, was obvious, from that first evening we walked together down the crowded tarmac road. If he had shouted it from the housetops, it could not have been more widely publicised—'Hands off Sarah!' And I was immensely grateful for his protection. There were so many ways of enticing a woman to surrender herself, and a locked bedroom door was no assurance of safety!

The sex taboo of my sheltered adolescence had left its mark on my adult awareness of sex. It was impossible to regard it with the careless and blatant mockery of so many of my contemporaries. To me, it was still a mystery, still a little vulgar, in spite of my earnest desire to have it otherwise. To arouse passion in a man was not my intention, for I had seen the unhappy result once before, and it had frightened me.

Yet I *was* intense, and the man beside me was intense. It was the most mutual and the most certain intensity I had ever known. Without any contact, other than a hand-clasp, this disturbing spark was smouldering in the depths of our two separate personalities. His bigness accentuated my smallness. My head barely reached his shoulder, and I was dwarfed by his towering strength. Without the arrogance, I found him extremely kind and understanding. We would talk of everything under the sun, except the one absorbing truth—that we were hopelessly and desperately in love. But beneath and beyond the essence of our love, respect and admiration, we ceased to think alike and were strangers.

'You would never believe my ignorance, Sarah, regarding all this,' said Paul, one evening, waving a cigarette at the surrounding countryside. His eyes twinkled, and he squeezed my hand affectionately. 'As you've probably noticed, my dear, I'm a gregarious sort of person, not given to isolation or meditation. Frankly, the country bores me, or did, till I met you! Who else could persuade me into leaning on a gate for the best part of an hour, staring at nothing but a few old apple trees, and an ugly mound of hills?'

'Ugly? Those hills? What's your idea of beauty, then?' I demanded.

'A city, blazing with lights. A dish of red salmon, garnished with cucumber. And a wine glass bubbling with champagne!' He laughed down at my incredulous face. 'It's the truth,' he insisted. 'I'm a city guy, and I've spent most of my adult life in cities—London, New York, Montreal, Manchester. Can you wonder I was scared to death when I saw this place?' he shuddered involuntarily. 'Then I saw you standing there in the doorway waiting to welcome me with such a jolly smile and suddenly it all clicked into place, and the pattern was explained. There is a pattern you know. Shall I tell you what you did for me that evening, Sarah? You saved me from a most deplorable state of self-pity. My wife and I had separated, and my company disintegrated with almost as big a bombshell! I was pretty desperate, I can tell you, and so completely engrossed in my own disaster I didn't give a thought to all the hundreds of thousands of others whose private little worlds had collapsed in ruins.' He sighed, and his searching eyes looking towards the hills saw nothing but devastation.

'Then you *were* bluffing, Paul?'

'Yes, I was bluffing,' he admitted.

'But I still don't understand what you saw in me. I'm so ordinary.'

'*Extra*ordinary!' he corrected—and now he was smiling again. 'My dear child, you are the most contradictory person I have ever met! I was intrigued to find such a diverting creature posing as a housemaid!'

'I am *not* posing as a housemaid. I am seriously engaged on work of national importance,' I reminded him, loftily. 'They told me so at the Ministry of Labour.'

'They didn't tell you that you would be expected to clean up after a gang of dirty, lazy ruffians, who ought to be ashamed of themselves!' he retorted.

'You have no right to criticise them, when you have obviously enjoyed all the advantages of environment and education, like the Major. This is their home for as long as the war lasts. It could be three months or three years, who knows? Well, I want it to be a home in the true sense of the word. Yes, I know I nag them, but that's my privilege. I'm getting fond of them, Paul. Don't you understand what I'm trying to say? I can put up with a bit of mess and muddle—I'm not terribly houseproud anyway—but I want them to be happy. I want *all* of you to be happy!'

'All right, Mamma, I'll be happy!' he teased. But his eyes seemed to contain some disappointment and he soon left me to join the Major and the boys.

*   *   *   *   *

At last he had spoken openly about his wife, turning his head to look down at me with that searching glance I found so disconcerting. I knew too that he was beginning to find leaning on a gate tedious, and my prejudices rather childish. His tenderness was not a natural instinct, but a cultivated one. Fundamentally he was forceful and dominant, and I knew now that he was only curbing his impatience by a rigid self-discipline. His very shape and size was suggestive of power and strength, not weakness, but his whole personality, with its gaiety and charm, was beginning to show a rather strained and disturbing quietness, like the calm before a storm.

I watched him walk down the long tarmac road, towards the main block of buildings, but his step was not so brisk, and he forgot to turn and wave to me, still standing at the gate. My heart contracted with an awful realization that he could ask for a transfer, and I should never see him again.

If this should happen I could not go on living here, for he had become so much a part of my life, it was impossible to imagine the place without him.

The hedges were draped in sweet-smelling blossoms. Bees hummed in the orchard. A blackbird sang exultantly from a high branch. In the beauty of the flowering spring all around me I was tormented by doubt.

'If Paul Taylor goes away there will never be another—

never!' I told myself. 'I couldn't bear to go through it all again! But what can I do? What is the answer? That one of us must go? That we tear ourselves apart before we have ever known each other as man and woman?'

I had fallen in love for the third and last time. Refusing to recognise reality only prolonged the pain. There was no escape for me, this time—*only by asking him to go.*

In the heart of the wood I sat down against the solid bulk of the old oak tree. I felt as small and insignificant as the early ladybird which settled on the back of my hand—colourful as a bead on a child's necklace—each tiny, black spot marked with perfect symmetry on its scarlet jacket.

'Fly away Peter! Fly away Paul!'

How many times had we chanted that old English rhyme, turning our skipping ropes, in the playground of the village school.

'Fly away Paul!'

The ladybird spread her wings, and disappeared into the shaft of sunlight filtering through the thick leafy branches.

Now I could not stop the tears, for the whole of me wept for the wasted years, that had taught me nothing.

And I wept because I was still a virgin.

This spark that was kindled between us, only a month ago, was mutual and spontaneous—a swift glance of recognition that completely extinguished the early loves. I had been tossed between pleasure and pain, thrilled and frightened. Never in my life had I known such heartache. Yet in the past month, I had matured beyond all recognition. Paul's un-English, unashamed 'courting' had reassured me and enabled me to grow at last.

With every leaping pulse I was listening now to the un-mistakable sound of snapping twigs under a heavy foot. I heard him calling 'Sarah! Sarah!' peremptorily, then suddenly gentle and persuasive—'Sweetheart, are you there?' He could be so gentle and persuasive when he chose, and the urge to get up and run into his arms was strong and compelling. He came to within a few yards of me, then saw me. We gazed at each other in silence for a while. I felt overwhelmed by the gravity of the situation, while Paul seemed untroubled by doubt or prejudice.

'I want you, Sarah, and you know it,' he said.

I could not ask him to go. My life seemed to have been directed to this place and this man. He felt it too, though he was not normally sensitive to intuition. The pattern, he said, is there, but we have to shape it ourselves, according to our needs and personalities. He had been amused by my fears that we were blown around like leaves in the wind, and only Chance saved us from disaster. Intuition was a woman's perogative, he said, and often landed her in a hell of a mess! Yet he was prepared to admit quite candidly that on this particular occasion he had not stopped to reason. He too had let intuition decide—on Somerset, and then, on me.

WAL